Especially for

_____

From

_____

Date

_____

THE
BIBLE
PROMISE
BOOK®

Inspired by the Bestselling Classic Devotional

GOD CALLING
EDITION

THE
BIBLE
PROMISE
BOOK®

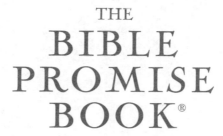

Inspired by the Bestselling Classic Devotional

GOD CALLING
EDITION

BARBOUR
PUBLISHING

Contents

Introduction

God's Word is full of promises.
And you know when He makes a promise,
you can trust it—always!

These inspiring Bible promises will challenge and encourage your soul!

Each topic in this promise book was inspired by the extraordinary classic devotional *God Calling*, edited by A. J. Russell, in which each devotional presents the thoughts of Jesus as if He is speaking directly to the reader.

Allow each scripture selection to speak to your heart as you draw ever closer to your heavenly Father.

The Publishers

All Is Well

I am thy shield. Have no fear. You must know that "all is well." I will never let anyone do to you both, other than My will for you.

I can see the future. I can read men's hearts. I know better than you what you need. Trust Me absolutely. You are not at the mercy of fate or buffeted about by others. You are being led in a very definite way, and others, who do not serve your purpose, are being moved out of your path by Me.

Never fear, whatever may happen. You are being led. Do not try to plan. I have planned. You are the builder, not the architect.

Go very quietly, very gently. All is for the very best for you.

Trust Me for all. Your very extremity will ensure My activity for you. And having your foundation on the Rock—Christ, faith in Him, and "being rooted and grounded in Him," and having belief in My divinity as your Cornerstone, it is yours to build, knowing all is well.

Literally, you have to depend on Me for everything— everything. It was out of the depths that David cried unto Me, and I heard his voice. All is well.

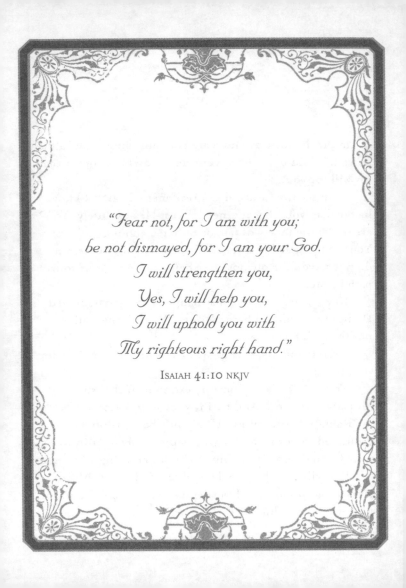

"Fear not, for I am with you;
be not dismayed, for I am your God.
I will strengthen you,
Yes, I will help you,
I will uphold you with
My righteous right hand."

ISAIAH 41:10 NKJV

For I am convinced that neither death nor life,
neither angels nor demons, neither the present nor the
future, nor any powers, neither height nor depth, nor
anything else in all creation, will be able to separate us
from the love of God that is in Christ Jesus our Lord.

ROMANS 8:38–39 NIV

"Whether it is favorable or unfavorable, we will obey the
LORD our God, to whom we are sending you, so that it will
go well with us, for we will obey the LORD our God."

JEREMIAH 42:6 NIV

"Give your entire attention to what God is doing
right now, and don't get worked up about what may or
may not happen tomorrow. God will help you deal with
whatever hard things come up when the time comes."

MATTHEW 6:34 MSG

"And why are you anxious about clothing? Consider
the lilies of the field, how they grow: they neither toil
nor spin, yet I tell you, even Solomon in all his glory
was not arrayed like one of these. But if God so clothes
the grass of the field, which today is alive and tomorrow
is thrown into the oven, will he not much
more clothe you, O you of little faith?"

MATTHEW 6:28–30 ESV

And my God will supply all your needs according to
His riches in glory in Christ Jesus. Now to our God
and Father be the glory forever and ever. Amen.

PHILIPPIANS 4:19–20 NASB

Yea, though I walk through the valley of the
shadow of death, I will fear no evil: for thou art
with me; thy rod and thy staff they comfort me.

PSALM 23:4 KJV

And we know that God causes all things to work
together for good to those who love God, to those
who are called according to His purpose.

ROMANS 8:28 NASB

"I have told you all this so that you may
have peace in me. Here on earth you will
have many trials and sorrows. But take heart,
because I have overcome the world."

JOHN 16:33 NLT

In peace I will lie down and sleep,
for you alone, LORD, make me dwell in safety.

PSALM 4:8 NIV

Whom have I in heaven but you? And earth
has nothing I desire besides you. My flesh
and my heart may fail, but God is the strength
of my heart and my portion forever.
PSALM 73:25–26 NIV

My people will live in peaceful dwelling places,
in secure homes, in undisturbed places of rest.
ISAIAH 32:18 NIV

Finally, brethren, farewell. Become complete.
Be of good comfort, be of one mind, live in peace;
and the God of love and peace will be with you.
2 CORINTHIANS 13:11 NKJV

The LORD gives his people strength.
The LORD blesses them with peace.
PSALM 29:11 NLT

May God our Father and the Lord Jesus
Christ give you grace and peace.
2 CORINTHIANS 1:2 NLT

God said to Moses, "I AM WHO I AM.
This is what you are to say to the Israelites:
'I AM has sent me to you.' "
EXODUS 3:14 NIV

"But the Helper, the Holy Spirit, whom
the Father will send in My name, He will
teach you all things, and bring to your
remembrance all things that I said to you."
JOHN 14:26 NKJV

When I am afraid, I put my trust in you.
PSALM 56:3 NIV

"Be strong and courageous. Do not be
afraid or terrified because of them, for the
LORD your God goes with you; he will never
leave you nor forsake you."
DEUTERONOMY 31:6 NIV

May the God of hope fill you with all joy and
peace as you trust in him, so that you may overflow
with hope by the power of the Holy Spirit.
ROMANS 15:13 NIV

And when I was burdened with worries,
you comforted me and made me feel secure.
PSALM 94:19 CEV

"But seek first his kingdom and his righteousness,
and all these things will be given to you as well."
MATTHEW 6:33 NIV

I will be with you always,
even until the end of the world.
MATTHEW 28:20 CEV

"Do not let your hearts be troubled.
You believe in God; believe also in me."
JOHN 14:1 NIV

So we say with confidence, "The Lord
is my helper; I will not be afraid.
What can mere mortals do to me?"
HEBREWS 13:6 NIV

Be careful to obey all these regulations I am giving you, so that it may always go well with you and your children after you, because you will be doing what is good and right in the eyes of the LORD your God.

DEUTERONOMY 12:28 NIV

"For the LORD your God is the one who goes with you to fight for you against your enemies to give you victory."

DEUTERONOMY 20:4 NIV

Seek good and not evil, that you may live; and thus may the LORD God of hosts be with you, just as you have said!

AMOS 5:14 NASB

The LORD thy God in the midst of thee is mighty; he will save, he will rejoice over thee with joy; he will rest in his love, he will joy over thee with singing.

ZEPHANIAH 3:17 KJV

Set your minds on things above, not on earthly
things. For you died, and your life is now hidden
with Christ in God. When Christ, who is your life,
appears, then you also will appear with him in glory.
COLOSSIANS 3:2–4 NIV

Keep your lives free from the love of money and be
content with what you have, because God has said,
"Never will I leave you; never will I forsake you."
HEBREWS 13:5 NIV

God is our refuge and strength,
a very present help in trouble.
PSALM 46:1 NASB

I will say of the LORD, He is my refuge and my
fortress: my God; in him will I trust.
PSALM 91:2 KJV

In the fear of the LORD is strong confidence:
and his children shall have a place of refuge.
PROVERBS 14:26 KJV

Jesus Christ is the same yesterday, today, and forever.
HEBREWS 13:8 NKJV

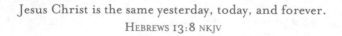

"The LORD himself goes before you and will
be with you; he will never leave you nor forsake you.
Do not be afraid; do not be discouraged."
DEUTERONOMY 31:8 NIV

"For you have been my hope, Sovereign LORD,
my confidence since my youth.
PSALM 71:5 NIV

All praise to God, the Father of our Lord Jesus
Christ. God is our merciful Father and the source
of all comfort. He comforts us in all our troubles
so that we can comfort others. When they are
troubled, we will be able to give them the
same comfort God has given us.
2 CORINTHIANS 1:3–4 NLT

"Do not be afraid of them, for I am with
you to deliver you," declares the LORD.
JEREMIAH 1:8 NASB

No one has ever seen God. But if we love
each other, God lives in us, and his love is
brought to full expression in us.

1 JOHN 4:12 NLT

"I know that You can do everything, and that no
purpose of Yours can be withheld from You."

JOB 42:2 NKJV

"The thief comes only to steal and kill and
destroy; I have come that they may have life,
and have it to the full."

JOHN 10:10 NIV

Bless the LORD, O my soul, and all that is
within me, bless his holy name! Bless the LORD,
O my soul, and forget not all his benefits,
who forgives all your iniquity, who heals all your
diseases, who redeems your life from the pit,
who crowns you with steadfast love and mercy,
who satisfies you with good so that your
youth is renewed like the eagle's.

PSALM 103:1–5 ESV

"Are not two sparrows sold for a penny?
And not one of them will fall to the ground apart
from your Father. But even the hairs of your
head are all numbered. Fear not, therefore;
you are of more value than many sparrows."
MATTHEW 10:29–31 ESV

I saw no temple in it, for the Lord God the Almighty
and the Lamb are its temple. And the city has no need
of the sun or of the moon to shine on it, for the glory
of God has illumined it, and its lamp is the Lamb.
The nations will walk by its light, and the kings
of the earth will bring their glory into it.
REVELATION 21:22–24 NASB

"In his hand is the life of every living
thing and the breath of all mankind."
JOB 12:10 ESV

This is the message we heard from Jesus
and now declare to you: God is light,
and there is no darkness in him at all.
1 JOHN 1:5 NLT

Blessings Are Yours

Listen, listen, I am your Lord. Before Me there is none other. Just trust Me in everything. Help is here all the time.

The difficult way is nearly over, but you have learned in it lessons you could learn in no other way. "The kingdom of heaven suffereth violence, and the violent take it by force." Wrest from Me, by firm and simple trust and persistent prayer, the treasures of My kingdom.

Such wonderful things are coming to you: joy—peace—assurance—security—health—happiness—laughter.

Claim big, really big, things now. Remember, nothing is too big. Satisfy the longing of My heart to give. Blessing, abundant blessing, on you both now and always. Peace.

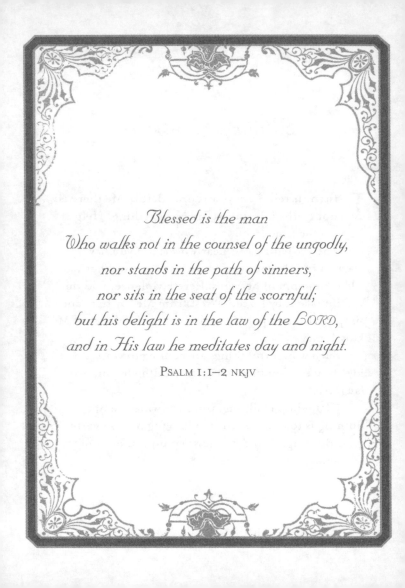

Blessed is the man
Who walks not in the counsel of the ungodly,
nor stands in the path of sinners,
nor sits in the seat of the scornful;
but his delight is in the law of the LORD,
and in His law he meditates day and night.

PSALM 1:1–2 NKJV

And my God shall supply all your need according
to His riches in glory by Christ Jesus.
PHILIPPIANS 4:19 NKJV

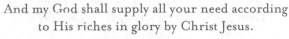

Praise be to the God and Father of our Lord Jesus
Christ, who has blessed us in the heavenly realms
with every spiritual blessing in Christ.
EPHESIANS 1:3 NIV

A faithful man will abound with blessings, but he who
makes haste to be rich will not go unpunished.
PROVERBS 28:20 NASB

"Bless those who curse you.
Pray for those who hurt you."
LUKE 6:28 NLT

Passing through the valley of Baca they make it a
spring; the early rain also covers it with blessings.
PSALM 84:6 NASB

I want to see you and share with you the same
blessings that God's Spirit has given me.
Then you will grow stronger in your faith.
ROMANS 1:11 CEV

Then He lifted up His eyes toward His
disciples, and said: "Blessed are you poor,
for yours is the kingdom of God."
LUKE 6:20 NKJV

You Gentiles are like branches of a wild olive tree that
were made to be part of a cultivated olive tree. You have
taken the place of some branches that were cut away
from it. And because of this, you enjoy the blessings
that come from being part of that cultivated tree.
ROMANS 11:17 CEV

Long ago the Scriptures said that God would accept
the Gentiles because of their faith. That's why God
told Abraham the good news that all nations would
be blessed because of him. This means that everyone
who has faith will share in the blessings that were
given to Abraham because of his faith.
GALATIANS 3:8–9 CEV

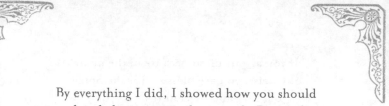

By everything I did, I showed how you should
work to help everyone who is weak. Remember
that our Lord Jesus said, "More blessings come
from giving than from receiving."

ACTS 20:35 CEV

I thank my God always concerning you for the grace of
God which was given to you by Christ Jesus, that you
were enriched in everything by Him in all utterance
and all knowledge, even as the testimony of Christ was
confirmed in you, so that you come short in no gift,
eagerly waiting for the revelation of our Lord Jesus
Christ, who will also confirm you to the end, that you
may be blameless in the day of our Lord Jesus Christ.

1 CORINTHIANS 1:4–8 NKJV

My prayer is that light will flood your hearts
and that you will understand the hope that was
given to you when God chose you. Then you will
discover the glorious blessings that will be yours
together with all of God's people.

EPHESIANS 1:18 CEV

If you are insulted because of the name
of Christ, you are blessed, for the Spirit
of glory and of God rests on you.

1 PETER 4:14 NIV

But whoever looks intently into the perfect
law that gives freedom, and continues
in it—not forgetting what they have heard,
but doing it—they will be blessed in what they do.

JAMES 1:25 NIV

But God has given us his Spirit. That's why we
don't think the same way that the people of
this world think. That's also why we can
recognize the blessings that God has given us.

1 CORINTHIANS 2:12 CEV

I became a servant of this gospel by the gift of God's
grace given me through the working of his power.
Although I am less than the least of all the Lord's people,
this grace was given me: to preach to the Gentiles
the boundless riches of Christ, and to make plain to
everyone the administration of this mystery, which for
ages past was kept hidden in God, who created all things.

EPHESIANS 3:7–9 NIV

He said to me: "It is done. I am the Alpha and the Omega, the Beginning and the End. To the thirsty I will give water without cost from the spring of the water of life. Those who are victorious will inherit all this, and I will be their God and they will be my children."

REVELATION 21:6–7 NIV

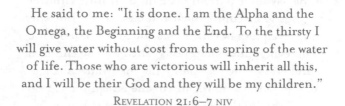

So God created human beings in his own image. In the image of God he created them; male and female he created them. Then God blessed them and said, "Be fruitful and multiply. Fill the earth and govern it. Reign over the fish in the sea, the birds in the sky, and all the animals that scurry along the ground."

GENESIS 1:27–28 NLT

"Blessed are you who hunger now, for you shall be satisfied. Blessed are you who weep now, for you shall laugh. Blessed are you when men hate you, and ostracize you, and insult you, and scorn your name as evil, for the sake of the Son of Man. Be glad in that day and leap for joy, for behold, your reward is great in heaven."

LUKE 6:21–23 NASB

One day some parents brought their little children
to Jesus so he could touch and bless them. But when
the disciples saw this, they scolded the parents for
bothering him. Then Jesus called for the children
and said to the disciples, "Let the children come
to me. Don't stop them! For the Kingdom of God
belongs to those who are like these children."

LUKE 18:15–16 NLT

"My Lord and my God!" Thomas exclaimed.
Then Jesus told him, "You believe because you have seen
me. Blessed are those who believe without seeing me."

JOHN 20:28–29 NLT

Every good and perfect gift is from above,
coming down from the Father of the heavenly lights,
who does not change like shifting shadows.

JAMES 1:17 NIV

"Give, and it will be given to you. A good measure,
pressed down, shaken together and running over,
will be poured into your lap. For with the measure
you use, it will be measured to you."

LUKE 6:38 NIV

The righteous lead blameless lives;
blessed are their children after them.
PROVERBS 20:7 NIV

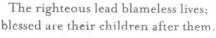

Whoever gives heed to instruction prospers,
and blessed is the one who trusts in the LORD.
PROVERBS 16:20 NIV

Blessed is the man that doeth this, and the son of man
that layeth hold on it; that keepeth the sabbath from
polluting it, and keepeth his hand from doing any evil.
ISAIAH 56:2 KJV

"Blessed are those who mourn,
for they will be comforted."
MATTHEW 5:4 NIV

But whoever looks intently into the perfect
law that gives freedom, and continues in it—
not forgetting what they have heard, but doing
it—they will be blessed in what they do.
JAMES 1:25 NIV

I always thank my God when I pray for you,
Philemon, because I keep hearing about your faith
in the Lord Jesus and your love for all of God's
people. And I am praying that you will put into action
the generosity that comes from your faith as you
understand and experience all the good things we
have in Christ. Your love has given me much joy
and comfort, my brother, for your kindness has
often refreshed the hearts of God's people.

PHILEMON 1:4–7 NLT

Children are a heritage from the LORD,
offspring a reward from him.
PSALM 127:3 NIV

"So I say to you; Ask and it will be given to you;
seek and you will find; knock and the door will be
opened to you. For everyone who asks receives;
the one who seeks finds; and to the one who
knocks, the door will be opened."
LUKE 11:9–10 NIV

You are wonderful, and while everyone watches,
you store up blessings for all who honor and trust
you. You are their shelter from harmful plots,
and you are their protection from vicious gossip.
PSALM 31:19–20 CEV

"Do not store up for yourselves treasures on earth,
where moths and vermin destroy, and where thieves
break in and steal. But store up for yourselves
treasures in heaven, where moths and vermin do not
destroy, and where thieves do not break in and steal.
For where your treasure is, there your heart will be also."
MATTHEW 6:19–21 NIV

"So when you give to the needy, do not announce it
with trumpets, as the hypocrites do in the synagogues
and on the streets, to be honored by others. Truly I
tell you, they have received their reward in full."
MATTHEW 6:2 NIV

A wicked person earns deceptive wages, but the
one who sows righteousness reaps a sure reward.
PROVERBS 11:18 NIV

Depend on Me

Rely on Me alone. Ask no other help. Pay all out in the spirit of trust that more will come to meet your supply.

Empty your vessels quickly to ensure a divine supply.

So much retained by you, so much the less will be gained from Me. It is a Law of Divine Supply.

To hold back, to retain, implies a fear of the future, a want of trust in Me.

When you ask Me to save you from the sea of poverty and difficulty, you must trust wholly to Me. If you do not, and your prayer and faith are genuine, then I must first answer your prayer for help as a rescuer does that of a drowning man who is struggling to save himself.

He renders him still more helpless and powerless until he is wholly at the will and mercy of the rescuer. So understand My leading. Trust wholly. Trust completely.

Empty your vessel. I will fill it. You ask both of you to understand divine supply. It is a most difficult lesson for My children to learn. So dependent have they become on material supply they fail to understand. You must live as I tell you.

Depend on Me.

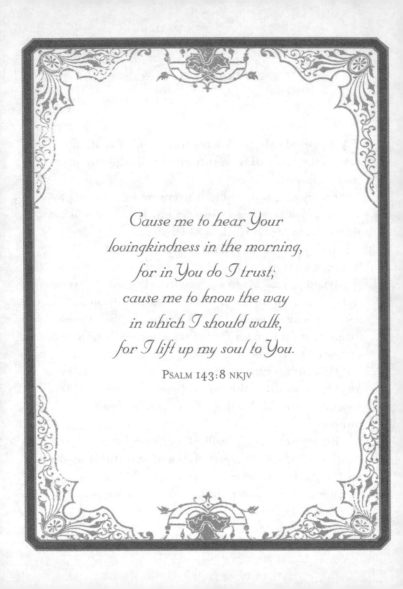

*Cause me to hear Your
lovingkindness in the morning,
for in You do I trust;
cause me to know the way
in which I should walk,
for I lift up my soul to You.*

PSALM 143:8 NKJV

Some trust in chariots and some in horses,
but we trust in the name of the LORD our God.

PSALM 20:7 NIV

LORD All-Powerful, you are God. You have
promised me some very good things, and you
can be trusted to do what you promise.

2 SAMUEL 7:28 CEV

But I am like an olive tree, thriving in the house
of God. I will always trust in God's unfailing love.
I will praise you forever, O God, for what you
have done. I will trust in your good name in
the presence of your faithful people.

PSALM 52:8–9 NLT

You make our hearts glad because
we trust you, the only God.

PSALM 33:21 CEV

But I am trusting you, O LORD, saying,
"You are my God!" My future is in your hands.
PSALM 31:14–15 NLT

O LORD, I give my life to you. I trust in you,
my God! Do not let me be disgraced, or let my
enemies rejoice in my defeat. No one who trusts
in you will ever be disgraced, but disgrace comes
to those who try to deceive others.
PSALM 25:1–3 NLT

"Do not put your trust in idols or make metal images
of gods for yourselves. I am the LORD your God."
LEVITICUS 19:4 NLT

He lifted me out of the pit of despair, out of the
mud and the mire. He set my feet on solid ground
and steadied me as I walked along. He has given me
a new song to sing, a hymn of praise to our God.
Many will see what he has done and be amazed.
They will put their trust in the LORD.
PSALM 40:2–3 NLT

My victory and honor come from God alone.
He is my refuge, a rock where no enemy can reach
me. O my people, trust in him at all times. Pour
out your heart to him, for God is our refuge.
PSALM 62:7–8 NLT

"Don't let your hearts be troubled.
Trust in God, and trust also in me."
JOHN 14:1 NLT

May the God of hope fill you with all joy and
peace as you trust in him, so that you may overflow
with hope by the power of the Holy Spirit.
ROMANS 15:13 NIV

In that day the people will proclaim, "This is
our God! We trusted in him, and he saved us!
This is the LORD, in whom we trusted. Let us
rejoice in the salvation he brings!"
ISAIAH 25:9 NLT

Let us hold unswervingly to the hope we profess,
for he who promised is faithful.
HEBREWS 10:23 NIV

I pray that from his glorious, unlimited resources
he will empower you with inner strength through his
Spirit. Then Christ will make his home in your hearts
as you trust in him. Your roots will grow down into
God's love and keep you strong. And may you have the
power to understand, as all God's people should, how
wide, how long, how high, and how deep his love is.
EPHESIANS 3:16—18 NLT

Surely the righteous will never be shaken; they will be
remembered forever. They will have no fear of bad
news; their hearts are steadfast, trusting in the LORD.
Their hearts are secure, they will have no fear; in the
end they will look in triumph on their foes.
PSALM 112:6—8 NIV

And so we know and rely on the love God
has for us. God is love. Whoever lives in
love lives in God, and God in them.
1 JOHN 4:16 NIV

And this same God who takes care of me will
supply all your needs from his glorious riches,
which have been given to us in Christ Jesus.
PHILIPPIANS 4:19 NLT

Trust in the LORD, and do good; dwell in
the land and befriend faithfulness.
PSALM 37:3 ESV

Keep your life free from love of money,
and be content with what you have, for
he has said, "I will never leave you nor
forsake you." So we can confidently say,
"The Lord is my helper; I will not fear;
what can man do to me?"
HEBREWS 13:5–6 ESV

All Scripture is inspired by God and profitable for
teaching, for reproof, for correction, for training
in righteousness; so that the man of God may be
adequate, equipped for every good work.
2 TIMOTHY 3:16–17 NASB

Whoever trusts in his own mind is a fool,
but he who walks in wisdom will be delivered.
PROVERBS 28:26 ESV

"Nor is there salvation in any other,
for there is no other name under heaven
given among men by which we must be saved."
ACTS 4:12 NKJV

Oh, taste and see that the LORD is good!
Blessed is the man who takes refuge in him!
PSALM 34:8 ESV

I will wait for the LORD, who is hiding his face from
the descendants of Jacob. I will put my trust in him.
ISAIAH 8:17 NIV

Trust in the LORD with all your heart
and do not lean on your own understanding.
In all your ways acknowledge Him,
and He will make your paths straight.

PROVERBS 3:5–6 NASB

In you our ancestors put their trust; they trusted and
you delivered them. To you they cried out and were
saved; in you they trusted and were not put to shame.

PSALM 22:4–5 NIV

Respect the LORD your God, serve only him,
and make promises in his name alone.

DEUTERONOMY 10:20 CEV

For all the promises of God in Him are Yes, and in
Him Amen, to the glory of God through us. Now
He who establishes us with you in Christ and has
anointed us is God, who also has sealed us and
given us the Spirit in our hearts as a guarantee.

2 CORINTHIANS 1:20–22 NKJV

"No one has ever gone up into the presence of
God except the One who came down from that
Presence, the Son of Man. In the same way that
Moses lifted the serpent in the desert so people
could have something to see and then believe,
it is necessary for the Son of Man to be lifted up—
and everyone who looks up to him, trusting and
expectant, will gain a real life, eternal life."
JOHN 3:13–15 MSG

And the Lord said, "If you had faith like a
mustard seed, you would say to this mulberry
tree, 'Be uprooted and be planted
in the sea'; and it would obey you."
LUKE 17:6 NASB

I praise your promises! I trust you and
am not afraid. No one can harm me.
PSALM 56:4 CEV

Don't forget how the LORD your God has led you through the desert for the past forty years. He wanted to find out if you were truly willing to obey him and depend on him, so he made you go hungry. Then he gave you manna, a kind of food that you and your ancestors had never even heard about. The LORD was teaching you that people need more than food to live—they need every word that the LORD has spoken.

DEUTERONOMY 8:2–3 CEV

So Moses and Aaron proceeded to round up all the leaders of Israel. Aaron told them everything that GOD had told Moses and demonstrated the wonders before the people. And the people trusted and listened believingly that GOD was concerned with what was going on with the Israelites and knew all about their affliction. They bowed low and they worshiped.

EXODUS 4:29–31 MSG

This is why the fulfillment of God's promise
depends entirely on trusting God and his way, and
then simply embracing him and what he does. God's
promise arrives as pure gift. That's the only way
everyone can be sure to get in on it, those who keep
the religious traditions *and* those who have never heard
of them. For Abraham is father of us all. He is not
our racial father—that's reading the story backwards.
He is our *faith* father.

ROMANS 4:16 MSG

"Behold, the man who would not make God his
refuge, but trusted in the abundance of his
riches and was strong in his evil desire."

PSALM 52:7 NASB

Trust in him at all times, you people; pour out
your hearts to him, for God is our refuge.

PSALM 62:8 NIV

I Am Love

L ove and fear cannot dwell together. By their very natures they cannot exist side by side. Evil is powerful, and fear is one of evil's most potent forces.

Therefore a weak, vacillating love can be soon routed by fear, whereas a perfect love, a trusting love, is immediately the conqueror, and fear, vanquished, flees in confusion.

But I am love because God is love, and I and the Father are one. So the only way to obtain this perfect love, that dispels fear, is to have Me more and more in your lives. You can only banish fear by My presence and My name.

Fear of the future—Jesus will be with us.

Fear of poverty—Jesus will provide. (And so to all the temptations of fear.)

You must not allow fear to enter. Talk to Me. Think of Me. Talk of Me. Love Me. And that sense of My power will so possess you that no fear can possess your mind. Be strong in this My love.

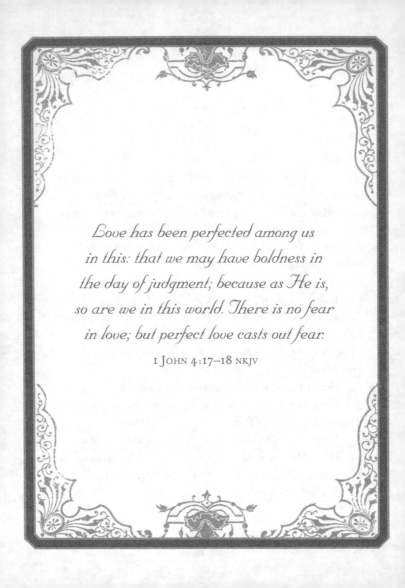

*Love has been perfected among us
in this: that we may have boldness in
the day of judgment; because as He is,
so are we in this world. There is no fear
in love; but perfect love casts out fear.*

I JOHN 4:17–18 NKJV

He who does not love does not
know God, for God is love.
1 JOHN 4:8 NKJV

But as it is written: "Eye has not seen, nor ear heard,
nor have entered into the heart of man the things
which God has prepared for those who love Him."
1 CORINTHIANS 2:9 NKJV

And we have known and believed the love that
God has for us. God is love, and he who abides
in love abides in God, and God in him.
1 JOHN 4:16 NKJV

But whoso keepeth his word, in him verily is the love
of God perfected: hereby know we that we are in him.
1 JOHN 2:5 KJV

"And you must love the LORD your
God with all your heart, all your soul,
all your mind, and all your strength."
MARK 12:30 NLT

"I call heaven and earth as witnesses today against you, that I have set before you life and death, blessing and cursing; therefore choose life, that both you and your descendants may live; that you may love the LORD your God, that you may obey His voice, and that you may cling to Him, for He is your life and the length of your days; and that you may dwell in the land which the LORD swore to your fathers, to Abraham, Isaac, and Jacob, to give them."

DEUTERONOMY 30:19–20 NKJV

But God, who is rich in mercy, because of His great love with which He loved us, even when we were dead in trespasses, made us alive together with Christ (by grace you have been saved), and raised us up together, and made us sit together in the heavenly places in Christ Jesus, that in the ages to come He might show the exceeding riches of His grace in His kindness toward us in Christ Jesus.

EPHESIANS 2:4–7 NKJV

For this is the love of God, that we keep His commandments. And His commandments are not burdensome.

1 JOHN 5:3 NKJV

This is how God showed his love among us: He sent his one and only Son into the world that we might live through him. This is love: not that we loved God, but that he loved us and sent his Son as an atoning sacrifice for our sins. Dear friends, since God so loved us, we also ought to love one another.

1 JOHN 4:9–11 NIV

"For God loved the world so much that he gave his one and only Son, so that everyone who believes in him will not perish but have eternal life."

JOHN 3:16 NLT

But God showed how much he loved us by having Christ die for us, even though we were sinful.

ROMANS 5:8 CEV

The LORD thy God in the midst of thee is mighty; he will save, he will rejoice over thee with joy; he will rest in his love, he will joy over thee with singing.

ZEPHANIAH 3:17 KJV

But you, Lord, are a compassionate
and gracious God, slow to anger,
abounding in love and faithfulness.

PSALM 86:15 NIV

See what great love the Father has lavished on us,
that we should be called children of God! And that
is what we are! The reason the world does not
know us is that it did not know him.

1 JOHN 3:1 NIV

"I love those who love me; and those
who diligently seek me will find me."

PROVERBS 8:17 NASB

"A new commandment I give to you, that you love one
another, even as I have loved you, that you also love
one another. By this all men will know that you are
My disciples, if you have love for one another."

JOHN 13:34—35 NASB

Love never fails. But where there are prophecies, they will cease; where there are tongues, they will be stilled; where there is knowledge, it will pass away. For we know in part and we prophesy in part, but when completeness comes, what is in part disappears. When I was a child, I talked like a child, I thought like a child, I reasoned like a child. When I became a man, I put the ways of childhood behind me. For now we see only a reflection as in a mirror; then we shall see face to face. Now I know in part; then I shall know fully, even as I am fully known. And now these three remain: faith, hope and love. But the greatest of these is love.

1 CORINTHIANS 13:8–13 NIV

Always be humble and gentle. Be patient with each other, making allowance for each other's faults because of your love. Make every effort to keep yourselves united in the Spirit, binding yourselves together with peace.

EPHESIANS 4:2–3 NLT

No, in all these things we are more than conquerors through him who loved us. For I am convinced that neither death nor life, neither angels nor demons, neither the present nor the future, nor any powers, neither height nor depth, nor anything else in all creation, will be able to separate us from the love of God that is in Christ Jesus our Lord.

ROMANS 8:37–39 NIV

You were cleansed from your sins when you obeyed the truth, so now you must show sincere love to each other as brothers and sisters. Love each other deeply with all your heart.

1 PETER 1:22 NLT

"You have heard the law that says, 'Love your neighbor' and hate your enemy. But I say, love your enemies! Pray for those who persecute you! In that way, you will be acting as true children of your Father in heaven. For he gives his sunlight to both the evil and the good, and he sends rain on the just and the unjust alike."

MATTHEW 5:43–45 NLT

I will be glad and rejoice in your love, for you saw
my affliction and knew the anguish of my soul.
You have not given me into the hands of the enemy
but have set my feet in a spacious place.
PSALM 31:7–8 NIV

He loves righteousness and justice; the earth
is full of the lovingkindness of the LORD.
PSALM 33:5 NASB

Your love, LORD, reaches to the heavens,
your faithfulness to the skies.
PSALM 36:5 NIV

"For the mountains may move and the hills disappear,
but even then my faithful love for you will remain.
My covenant of blessing will never be broken,"
says the LORD, who has mercy on you.
ISAIAH 54:10 NLT

Because of the LORD's great love we are not
consumed, for his compassions never fail. They
are new every morning; great is your faithfulness.
LAMENTATIONS 3:22–23 NIV

But the fruit of the Spirit is love, joy, peace,
forbearance, kindness, goodness, faithfulness,
gentleness and self-control. Against such
things there is no law.
GALATIANS 5:22–23 NIV

For the LORD corrects those he loves, just as
a father corrects a child in whom he delights.
PROVERBS 3:12 NLT

O may Your lovingkindness comfort me,
according to Your word to Your servant.
PSALM 119:76 NASB

I have been crucified with Christ; and it is no longer
I who live, but Christ lives in me; and the life which I
now live in the flesh I live by faith in the Son of God,
who loved me and gave Himself up for me.
GALATIANS 2:20 NASB

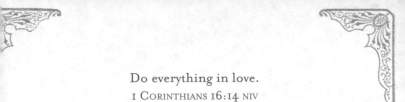

Do everything in love.
1 CORINTHIANS 16:14 NIV

And I pray that you, being rooted and established
in love, may have power, together with all the Lord's
holy people, to grasp how wide and long and high and
deep is the love of Christ, and to know this love that
surpasses knowledge—that you may be filled to the
measure of all the fullness of God.
EPHESIANS 3:17–19 NIV

I will instruct you and teach you in the way you should
go; I will counsel you with my loving eye on you.
PSALM 32:8 NIV

The blameless spend their days under the LORD's care,
and their inheritance will endure forever.
PSALM 37:18 NIV

Come, let us bow down in worship, let us kneel before
the LORD our Maker; for he is our God and we are the
people of his pasture, the flock under his care.
PSALM 95:6–7 NIV

But the wisdom that comes from heaven is first of all
pure; then peace-loving, considerate, submissive,
full of mercy and good fruit, impartial and sincere.
JAMES 3:17 NIV

You give great victories to your king;
you show unfailing love to your anointed,
to David and all his descendants forever.
PSALM 18:50 NLT

Remember, O LORD, your compassion and unfailing
love, which you have shown from long ages past.
Do not remember the rebellious sins of my youth.
Remember me in the light of your unfailing love,
for you are merciful, O LORD.
PSALM 25:6–7 NLT

Make Your face to shine upon Your servant;
save me in Your lovingkindness.
PSALM 31:16 NASB

I Am Your Guide

I am beside you. Follow in all things My guiding.
Marvels beyond all your imaginings are unfolding.
I am your Guide. Joy in that thought. Your Guide
and your Friend.

Remember that to Me a miracle is only a natural
happening. To My disciples, to My chosen, a miracle is
only a natural happening. But it is a natural happening
operative through spiritual forces, and therefore the
man who works and understands through the senses
only regards it as something contrary to nature.

My children, the children of My kingdom, are a
peculiar people, set apart, with different hopes and
aspirations and motives and sense of reward.

You see a marvelous happening (as that today),
happening so easily, so simply, so free from all other
agency, and you wonder.

My children, listen, this has not happened easily
and simply. It has been achieved by hours, days,
months of weariness and heartache battled against
and overcome by a steadfast, unflinching desire to
conquer self and to do My will and live My teachings.

The frets and the worries and the scorn patiently
borne mean spiritual power acquired, operating
marvelously.

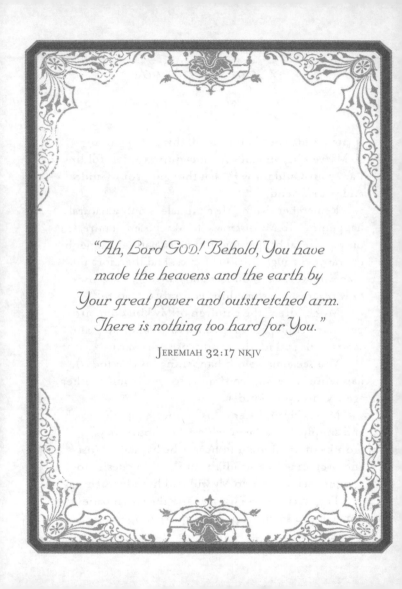

"Ah, Lord GOD! Behold, You have made the heavens and the earth by Your great power and outstretched arm. There is nothing too hard for You."

JEREMIAH 32:17 NKJV

"I myself will tend my sheep and have them
lie down, declares the Sovereign LORD."
EZEKIEL 34:15 NIV

He makes me lie down in green pastures; He leads me
beside quiet waters. He restores my soul; He guides
me in the paths of righteousness for His name's sake.
PSALM 23:2–3 NASB

"In Your lovingkindness You have led the people
whom You have redeemed; in Your strength
You have guided them to Your holy habitation."
EXODUS 15:13 NASB

For You are my rock and my fortress; for Your
name's sake You will lead me and guide me.
You will pull me out of the net which they have
secretly laid for me, for You are my strength.
PSALM 31:3–4 NASB

He tends his flock like a shepherd: He gathers the
lambs in his arms and carries them close to his heart;
he gently leads those that have young.

ISAIAH 40:11 NIV

Your word is a lamp for my feet, a light on my path.
I have taken an oath and confirmed it,
that I will follow your righteous laws.

PSALM 119:105–106 NIV

Yet I am always with you; you hold me by my right
hand. You guide me with your counsel, and afterward
you will take me into glory. Whom have I in heaven
but you? And earth has nothing I desire besides you.

PSALM 73:23–25 NIV

The LORD is my shepherd, I lack nothing.

PSALM 23:1 NIV

For a child will be born to us, a son will be given to
us; and the government will rest on His shoulders;
and His name will be called Wonderful Counselor,
Mighty God, Eternal Father, Prince of Peace.

ISAIAH 9:6 NASB

For this God is our God for ever and ever;
he will be our guide even to the end.
PSALM 48:14 NIV

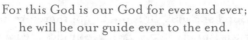

"I will lead the blind by ways they have not known,
along unfamiliar paths I will guide them; I will turn
the darkness into light before them and make the
rough places smooth. These are the things I will do;
I will not forsake them."
ISAIAH 42:16 NIV

I have kept my feet from every evil
path so that I might obey your word.
PSALM 119:101 NIV

Thomas said to him, "Lord, we don't know where
you are going, so how can we know the way?" Jesus
answered, "I am the way and the truth and the life.
No one comes to the Father except through me.
If you really know me, you will know my Father as well.
From now on, you do know him and have seen him."
JOHN 14:5–7 NIV

Good and upright is the LORD; therefore he instructs sinners in his ways. He guides the humble in what is right and teaches them his way. All the ways of the LORD are loving and faithful toward those who keep the demands of his covenant.

PSALM 25:8–10 NIV

But he brought his people out like a flock; he led them like sheep through the wilderness. He guided them safely, so they were unafraid; but the sea engulfed their enemies. And so he brought them to the border of his holy land, to the hill country his right hand had taken.

PSALM 78:52–54 NIV

"Never again will they hunger; never again will they thirst. The sun will not beat down on them," nor any scorching heat. For the Lamb at the center of the throne will be their shepherd; "he will lead them to springs of living water." "And God will wipe away every tear from their eyes."

REVELATION 7:16–17 NIV

Trust in the LORD with all thine heart; and
lean not unto thine own understanding. In all
thy ways acknowledge him, and he shall direct
thy paths. Be not wise in thine own eyes:
fear the LORD, and depart from evil.

PROVERBS 3:5–7 KJV

The mind of man plans his way,
but the LORD directs his steps.

PROVERBS 16:9 NASB

Know that the LORD is God. It is he who made us, and
we are his; we are his people, the sheep of his pasture.

PSALM 100:3 NIV

"I am the door, and the person who enters
through me will be saved and will be able
to come in and go out and find pasture."

JOHN 10:9 NCV

I know, O LORD, that a man's way is not in himself,
nor is it in a man who walks to direct his steps.

JEREMIAH 10:23 NASB

"I will multiply your descendants as the stars of heaven,
and will give your descendants all these lands; and by
your descendants all the nations of the earth shall be
blessed; because Abraham obeyed Me and kept My
charge, My commandments, My statutes and My laws."

GENESIS 26:4–5 NASB

And do not be conformed to this world, but
be transformed by the renewing of your mind,
so that you may prove what the will of God is,
that which is good and acceptable and perfect.

ROMANS 12:2 NASB

So then, those who suffer according to God's
will should commit themselves to their faithful
Creator and continue to do good.

1 PETER 4:19 NIV

"But seek first His kingdom and His righteousness,
and all these things will be added to you."
MATTHEW 6:33 NASB

Make sure that nobody pays back wrong for
wrong, but always strive to do what is good for
each other and for everyone else. Rejoice always,
pray continually, give thanks in all circumstances;
for this is God's will for you in Christ Jesus.
1 THESSALONIANS 5:15–18 NIV

It is God's will that your honorable lives should
silence those ignorant people who make foolish
accusations against you. For you are free, yet you are
God's slaves, so don't use your freedom as an excuse
to do evil. Respect everyone, and love your Christian
brothers and sisters. Fear God, and respect the king.
1 PETER 2:15–17 NLT

"And when he brings out his own sheep,
he goes before them; and the sheep follow him,
for they know his voice. Yet they will by no
means follow a stranger, but will flee from him,
for they do not know the voice of strangers."

JOHN 10:4–5 NKJV

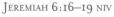

This is what the LORD says: "Stand at the crossroads
and look; ask for the ancient paths, ask where the
good way is, and walk in it, and you will find rest for
your souls. But you said, 'We will not walk in it.' I
appointed watchmen over you and said, 'Listen to
the sound of the trumpet!' But you said, 'We will not
listen.' Therefore hear, you nations; you who are
witnesses, observe what will happen to them. Hear,
you earth: I am bringing disaster on this people, the
fruit of their schemes, because they have not listened
to my words and have rejected my law."

JEREMIAH 6:16–19 NIV

"This is what the Lord GOD says: I, myself, will search for my sheep and take care of them. As a shepherd takes care of his scattered flock when it is found, I will take care of my sheep. I will save them from all the places where they were scattered on a cloudy and dark day."

EZEKIEL 34:11–12 NCV

"Those people will never be hungry again, and they will never be thirsty again. The sun will not hurt them, and no heat will burn them, because the Lamb at the center of the throne will be their shepherd. He will lead them to springs of water that give life. And God will wipe away every tear from their eyes."

REVELATION 7:16–17 NCV

Then he looked at those seated in a circle around him and said, "Here are my mother and my brothers! Whoever does God's will is my brother and sister and mother."

MARK 3:34–35 NIV

"But the Helper, the Holy Spirit, whom the
Father will send in My name, He will teach you
all things, and bring to your remembrance
all things that I said to you."
JOHN 14:26 NKJV

Be imitators of me, just as I also am of Christ.
Now I praise you because you remember me in
everything and hold firmly to the traditions,
just as I delivered them to you.
1 CORINTHIANS 11:1–2 NASB

Be imitators of me, just as I also am of Christ.
This means that anyone who belongs to
Christ has become a new person. The old
life is gone; a new life has begun!
2 CORINTHIANS 5:17 NLT

The godly are directed by honesty;
the wicked fall beneath their load of sin.
PROVERBS 11:5 NLT

I Give Eternal Life

Wait. Wonders are unfolding. Tremble with awe. No man can stand upon the threshold of eternity unshaken. I give unto you eternal life. A free gift, a wonderful gift—the life of the ages.

Silently comes the kingdom. No man can judge when it enters the heart of man, only in results. Listen quietly. Sometimes you may get no message. Meet thus all the same. You will absorb an atmosphere.

Cultivate silence. "God speaks in silences." A silence, a soft wind. Each can be a message to convey My meaning to the heart, though by no voice, or even word.

Each word or thought of yours can be like a pearl that you drop into the secret place of another heart, and in some hour of need, lo! the recipient finds the treasure and realizes for the first time its value.

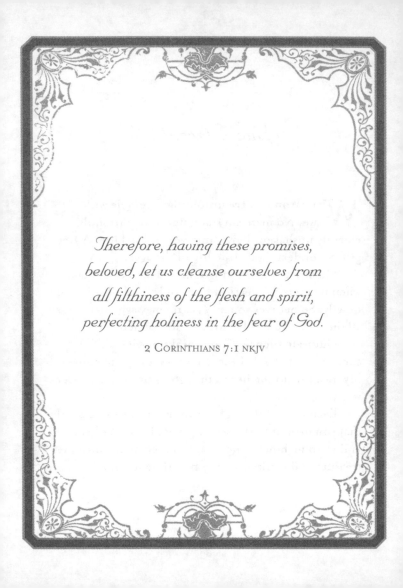

*Therefore, having these promises,
beloved, let us cleanse ourselves from
all filthiness of the flesh and spirit,
perfecting holiness in the fear of God.*

2 CORINTHIANS 7:1 NKJV

We know also that the Son of God has come and has
given us understanding, so that we may know him who
is true. And we are in him who is true by being in his
Son Jesus Christ. He is the true God and eternal life.

1 JOHN 5:20 NIV

※ ───※─※──⚘── ※─※─ ─※

After saying all these things, Jesus looked up to heaven
and said, "Father, the hour has come. Glorify your
Son so he can give glory back to you. For you have
given him authority over everyone. He gives eternal
life to each one you have given him. And this is the
way to have eternal life—to know you, the only true
God, and Jesus Christ, the one you sent to earth."

JOHN 17:1–3 NLT

※ ───※─※──⚘── ※─※─ ─※

God's law was given so that all people could see how
sinful they were. But as people sinned more and
more, God's wonderful grace became more abundant.
So just as sin ruled over all people and brought them
to death, now God's wonderful grace rules instead,
giving us right standing with God and resulting in
eternal life through Jesus Christ our Lord.

ROMANS 5:20–21 NLT

"Christ Jesus came into the world to save sinners."
This saying is true, and it can be trusted.
I was the worst sinner of all! But since I was
worse than anyone else, God had mercy on me and
let me be an example of the endless patience of
Christ Jesus. He did this so that others would put
their faith in Christ and have eternal life.

1 TIMOTHY 1:15–16 CEV

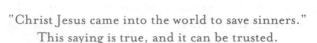

All who believe in the Son of God know in their
hearts that this testimony is true. Those who don't
believe this are actually calling God a liar because
they don't believe what God has testified about
his Son. And this is what God has testified: He
has given us eternal life, and this life is in his Son.
Whoever has the Son has life; whoever does
not have God's Son does not have life.

1 JOHN 5:10–12 NLT

72

Jesus replied, "I assure you that when the world is made new and the Son of Man sits upon his glorious throne, you who have been my followers will also sit on twelve thrones, judging the twelve tribes of Israel. And everyone who has given up houses or brothers or sisters or father or mother or children or property, for my sake, will receive a hundred times as much in return and will inherit eternal life."

MATTHEW 19:28–29 NLT

Blessed be the God and Father of our Lord Jesus Christ, who according to His great mercy has caused us to be born again to a living hope through the resurrection of Jesus Christ from the dead, to obtain an inheritance which is imperishable and undefiled and will not fade away, reserved in heaven for you, who are protected by the power of God through faith for a salvation ready to be revealed in the last time.

I PETER 1:3–5 NASB

"Just as Moses lifted up the snake in the wilderness, so the Son of Man must be lifted up, that everyone who believes may have eternal life in him." For God so loved the world that he gave his one and only Son, that whoever believes in him shall not perish but have eternal life.

JOHN 3:14–16 NIV

"My sheep listen to my voice; I know them, and they follow me. I give them eternal life, and they will never perish. No one can snatch them away from me, for my Father has given them to me, and he is more powerful than anyone else. No one can snatch them from the Father's hand."

JOHN 10:27–29 NLT

God showed his love for us when he sent his only Son into the world to give us life. Real love isn't our love for God, but his love for us. God sent his Son to be the sacrifice by which our sins are forgiven.

1 JOHN 4:9–10 CEV

My mouth is filled with GOD's praise.
Let everything living bless him,
bless his holy name from now to eternity!
PSALM 145:21 MSG

You therefore, beloved, knowing this beforehand, be
on your guard so that you are not carried away by the
error of unprincipled men and fall from your own
steadfastness, but grow in the grace and knowledge
of our Lord and Savior Jesus Christ. To Him be the
glory, both now and to the day of eternity. Amen.
2 PETER 3:17–18 NASB

"Truly I say to you, whatever you bind on earth shall
have been bound in heaven; and whatever you loose
on earth shall have been loosed in heaven."
MATTHEW 18:18 NASB

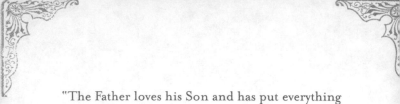

"The Father loves his Son and has put everything into his hands. And anyone who believes in God's Son has eternal life. Anyone who doesn't obey the Son will never experience eternal life but remains under God's angry judgment."

JOHN 3:35–36 NLT

"Do not let your heart be troubled; believe in God, believe also in Me. In My Father's house are many dwelling places; if it were not so, I would have told you; for I go to prepare a place for you. If I go and prepare a place for you, I will come again and receive you to Myself, that where I am, there you may be also."

JOHN 14:1–3 NASB

Just as people are destined to die once, and after that to face judgment, so Christ was sacrificed once to take away the sins of many; and he will appear a second time, not to bear sin, but to bring salvation to those who are waiting for him.

HEBREWS 9:27–28 NIV

"Do not marvel at this; for the hour is coming in which all who are in the graves will hear His voice and come forth—those who have done good, to the resurrection of life, and those who have done evil, to the resurrection of condemnation."

JOHN 5:28–29 NKJV

"Don't waste your energy striving for perishable food like that. Work for the food that sticks with you, food that nourishes your lasting life, food the Son of Man provides. He and what he does are guaranteed by God the Father to last."

JOHN 6:27 MSG

But you, dear friends, must build each other up in your most holy faith, pray in the power of the Holy Spirit, and await the mercy of our Lord Jesus Christ, who will bring you eternal life. In this way, you will keep yourselves safe in God's love. And you must show mercy to those whose faith is wavering.

JUDE 1:20–22 NLT

Jesus replied, "Anyone who drinks this water will soon become thirsty again. But those who drink the water I give will never be thirsty again. It becomes a fresh, bubbling spring within them, giving them eternal life."

JOHN 4:13–14 NLT

And he wants to make certain that none of the ones he has given me will be lost. Instead, he wants me to raise them to life on the last day. My Father wants everyone who sees the Son to have faith in him and to have eternal life. Then I will raise them to life on the last day.

JOHN 6:39–40 CEV

Then the Jews began to argue with one another, saying, "How can this man give us His flesh to eat?" So Jesus said to them, "Truly, truly, I say to you, unless you eat the flesh of the Son of Man and drink His blood, you have no life in yourselves. He who eats My flesh and drinks My blood has eternal life, and I will raise him up on the last day."

JOHN 6:52–54 NASB

Then Jesus turned to the Twelve and asked,
"Are you also going to leave?" Simon Peter replied,
"Lord, to whom would we go? You have the words
that give eternal life. We believe, and we know
you are the Holy One of God."
JOHN 6:67–69 NLT

"Very truly I tell you, whoever hears my word and
believes him who sent me has eternal life and will not
be judged but has crossed over from death to life.
Very truly I tell you, a time is coming and has now
come when the dead will hear the voice of the
Son of God and those who hear will live."
JOHN 5:24–25 NIV

"The Spirit gives life; the flesh counts for
nothing. The words I have spoken to you—
they are full of the Spirit and life."
JOHN 6:63 NIV

But God will rescue me
from the power of death.
PSALM 49:15 CEV

If I live, it will be for Christ, and if I die, I will gain
even more. I don't know what to choose. I could keep
on living and doing something useful. It is a hard
choice to make. I want to die and be with Christ,
because that would be much better. But I know that all
of you still need me. That's why I am sure I will stay
on to help you grow and be happy in your faith.
PHILIPPIANS 1:21–25 CEV

"I am the Living One; I was dead,
and now look, I am alive for ever and ever!
And I hold the keys of death and Hades."
REVELATION 1:18 NIV

Surely your goodness and love will follow
me all the days of my life, and I will dwell
in the house of the LORD forever.
PSALM 23:6 NIV

I Give You Hope

Your hope is in the Lord. More and more set your hopes on Me. Know that whatever the future may hold it will hold more and more of Me. It cannot but be glad and full of Joy. So in heaven, or on earth, wherever you may be, your way must be truly one of delight.

Do not try to find answers to the mysteries of the world. Learn to know Me more and more, and in that knowledge you will have all the answers you need here, and when you see Me face-to-face, in that purely spiritual world, you will find no need to ask. There again all your answers will be in Me.

Remember, I was the answer in time to all man's questions about My Father and His laws. Know no theology. Know Me. I was the Word of God. All you need to know about God you know in Me. If a man knows Me not, all your explanations will fall on an unresponsive heart.

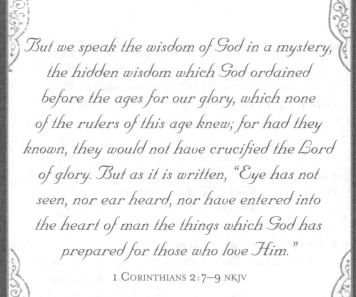

But we speak the wisdom of God in a mystery, the hidden wisdom which God ordained before the ages for our glory, which none of the rulers of this age knew; for had they known, they would not have crucified the Lord of glory. But as it is written, "Eye has not seen, nor ear heard, nor have entered into the heart of man the things which God has prepared for those who love Him."

1 CORINTHIANS 2:7–9 NKJV

He renews our hopes
and heals our bodies.
PSALM 147:3 CEV

I trust in you; do not let me be put to shame,
nor let my enemies triumph over me. No one who
hopes in you will ever be put to shame, but shame will
come on those who are treacherous without cause.
PSALM 25:2–3 NIV

But you must continue to believe this truth and stand
firmly in it. Don't drift away from the assurance
you received when you heard the Good News.
COLOSSIANS 1:23 NLT

Even youths grow tired and weary, and young
men stumble and fall; but those who hope in the
LORD will renew their strength. They will soar on
wings like eagles; they will run and not grow weary,
they will walk and not be faint.
ISAIAH 40:30–31 NIV

We wait in hope for the LORD; he is our help and our shield. In him our hearts rejoice, for we trust in his holy name.

PSALM 33:20–21 NIV

Not only so, but we also glory in our sufferings, because we know that suffering produces perseverance; perseverance, character; and character, hope. And hope does not put us to shame, because God's love has been poured out into our hearts through the Holy Spirit, who has been given to us.

ROMANS 5:3–5 NIV

The Spirit makes us sure about what we will be in the future. But now we groan silently, while we wait for God to show that we are his children. This means that our bodies will also be set free. And this hope is what saves us. But if we already have what we hope for, there is no need to keep on hoping. However, we hope for something we have not yet seen, and we patiently wait for it.

ROMANS 8:23–25 CEV

I pray that God, who gives hope, will bless
you with complete happiness and peace
because of your faith. And may the power
of the Holy Spirit fill you with hope.

ROMANS 15:13 CEV

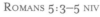

He will give eternal life to everyone who has patiently
done what is good in the hope of receiving glory,
honor, and life that lasts forever.

ROMANS 2:7 CEV

For what you have done I will always praise you in the
presence of your faithful people. And I will hope in
your name, for your name is good.

PSALM 52:9 NIV

Not only so, but we also glory in our sufferings,
because we know that suffering produces
perseverance; perseverance, character; and character,
hope. And hope does not put us to shame, because
God's love has been poured out into our hearts
through the Holy Spirit, who has been given to us.

ROMANS 5:3–5 NIV

Why, my soul, are you downcast? Why so disturbed
within me? Put your hope in God, for I will
yet praise him, my Savior and my God.
PSALM 42:5 NIV

The LORD All-Powerful will destroy the power of death
and wipe away all tears. No longer will his people be
insulted everywhere. The LORD has spoken! At that
time, people will say, "The LORD has saved us! Let's
celebrate. We waited and hoped—now our God is here."
ISAIAH 25:8–9 CEV

"But now, Lord, what do I look for?
My hope is in you."
PSALM 39:7 NIV

Even before sunrise, I pray for your help, and I put
my hope in what you have said. I lie awake at night,
thinking of your promises.
PSALM 119:147–148 CEV

But as for me, I watch in hope for the LORD,
I wait for God my Savior; my God will hear me.
MICAH 7:7 NIV

Hope in the LORD and keep his way. He will
exalt you to inherit the land; when the
wicked are destroyed, you will see it.

PSALM 37:34 NIV

I say to myself, "The LORD is my inheritance;
therefore, I will hope in him!"

LAMENTATIONS 3:24 NLT

For the earnest expectation of the creation eagerly
waits for the revealing of the sons of God. For the
creation was subjected to futility, not willingly,
but because of Him who subjected it in hope.

ROMANS 8:19–20 NKJV

And we desire that each one of you show the same
diligence to the full assurance of hope until the end,
that you do not become sluggish, but imitate those
who through faith and patience inherit the promises.

HEBREWS 6:11–12 NKJV

But the eyes of the LORD are on those who fear him,
on those whose hope is in his unfailing love, to deliver
them from death and keep them alive in famine.

PSALM 33:18–19 NIV

Let the peace of Christ rule in your hearts,
since as members of one body you were
called to peace. And be thankful.

COLOSSIANS 3:15 NIV

There is surely a future hope for you,
and your hope will not be cut off.

PROVERBS 23:18 NIV

When I made a sacred agreement with you, my people,
we sealed it with blood. Now some of you are captives
in waterless pits, but I will come to your rescue and
offer you hope. Return to your fortress, because today
I will reward you with twice what you had.

ZECHARIAH 9:11–12 CEV

I will bless you with a future filled with hope—
a future of success, not of suffering.
JEREMIAH 29:11 CEV

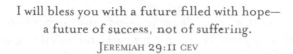

Though the fig tree should not blossom and there be
no fruit on the vines, though the yield of the olive
should fail and the fields produce no food, though
the flock should be cut off from the fold and there
be no cattle in the stalls, yet I will exult in the LORD,
I will rejoice in the God of my salvation. The Lord
GOD is my strength, and He has made my feet like
hinds' feet, and makes me walk on my high places.
HABAKKUK 3:17–19 NASB

Wait for the LORD; be strong and let your
heart take courage; yes, wait for the LORD.
PSALM 27:14 NASB

If only for this life we have hope in Christ,
we are of all people most to be pitied.
1 CORINTHIANS 15:19 NIV

My soul, wait in silence for God only, for my hope
is from Him. He only is my rock and my salvation,
my stronghold; I shall not be shaken.

PSALM 62:5–6 NASB

May integrity and uprightness protect me,
because my hope, LORD, is in you.

PSALM 25:21 NIV

And my speech and my preaching were not
with persuasive words of human wisdom,
but in demonstration of the Spirit and of power,
that your faith should not be in the wisdom
of men but in the power of God.

1 CORINTHIANS 2:4–5 NKJV

Consequently, faith comes from hearing
the message, and the message is heard
through the word about Christ.

ROMANS 10:17 NIV

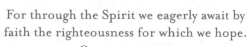

For through the Spirit we eagerly await by
faith the righteousness for which we hope.

GALATIANS 5:5 NIV

Show me your ways, LORD, teach me your paths.
Guide me in your truth and teach me, for you are
God my Savior, and my hope is in you all day long.
Remember, LORD, your great mercy and love,
for they are from of old.

PSALM 25:4–6 NIV

The wicked go down to the realm of the dead, all the
nations that forget God. But God will never forget the
needy; the hope of the afflicted will never perish.

PSALM 9:17–18 NIV

Therefore, since we are surrounded by such a
great cloud of witnesses, let us throw off everything
that hinders and the sin that so easily entangles. And
let us run with perseverance the race marked out for
us, fixing our eyes on Jesus, the pioneer and perfecter
of faith. For the joy set before him he endured the
cross, scorning its shame, and sat down at the
right hand of the throne of God.

HEBREWS 12:1–2 NIV

Bless the Lord, O my soul, and forget none of
His benefits; who pardons all your iniquities,
who heals all your diseases; who redeems your life
from the pit, who crowns you with lovingkindness and
compassion; who satisfies your years with good things,
so that your youth is renewed like the eagle.

Psalm 103:2–5 NASB

One thing I ask from the Lord, this only do
I seek: that I may dwell in the house of the Lord
all the days of my life, to gaze on the beauty
of the Lord and to seek him in his temple.
For in the day of trouble he will keep me safe
in his dwelling; he will hide me in the shelter
of his sacred tent and set me high upon a rock.

Psalm 27:4–5 NIV

I Give You Joy

Y ou have to hush the heart and bid all your senses
be still before you can be attuned to receive
heaven's music.

Your five senses are your means of communi-
cation with the material world, the links between
your real Spirit-life and the material manifestations
around you, but you must sever all connection with
them when you wish to hold Spirit-communication.
They will hinder, not help.

See the good in everybody. Love the good in
them. See your unworthiness compared with their
worth. Love, laugh, make the world, your little world,
happy.

As the ripples caused by a flung stone stir the
surface of a whole pond, so your joy-making shall
spread in ever-widening circles, beyond all your
knowledge, all anticipation. Joy in Me. Such joy is
eternal.

Centuries after, it is still bearing joy's precious
fruit.

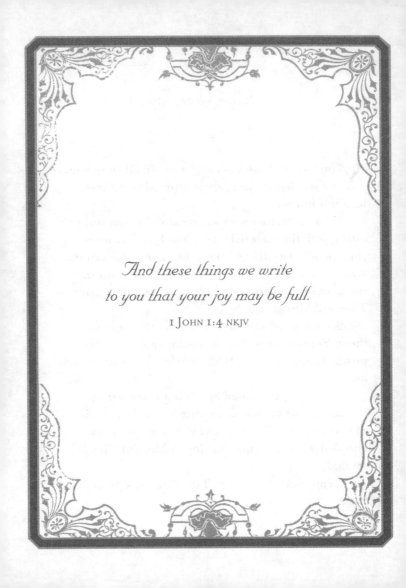

*And these things we write
to you that your joy may be full.*

1 JOHN 1:4 NKJV

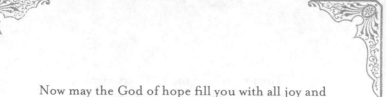

Now may the God of hope fill you with all joy and
peace in believing, so that you will abound in
hope by the power of the Holy Spirit.
ROMANS 15:13 NASB

After hearing the king, they went their way;
and the star, which they had seen in the east,
went on before them until it came and stood over
the place where the Child was. When they saw
the star, they rejoiced exceedingly with great joy.
MATTHEW 2:9–10 NASB

Then I will go to the altar of God, to God,
my joy and my delight. I will praise you
with the lyre, O God, my God.
PSALM 43:4 NIV

But the fruit of the Spirit is love, joy, peace, patience,
kindness, goodness, faithfulness, gentleness,
self-control; against such things there is no law.
GALATIANS 5:22–23 NASB

The precepts of the LORD are right,
giving joy to the heart. The commands of
the LORD are radiant, giving light to the eyes.
PSALM 19:8 NIV

I thank my God in all my remembrance of you,
always offering prayer with joy in my every prayer
for you all, in view of your participation in the
gospel from the first day until now.
PHILIPPIANS 1:3–5 NASB

God has ascended amid shouts of joy, the LORD amid
the sounding of trumpets. Sing praises to God,
sing praises; sing praises to our King, sing praises.
PSALM 47:5–6 NIV

Consider it all joy, my brethren, when you encounter
various trials, knowing that the testing of your
faith produces endurance. And let endurance have
its perfect result, so that you may be perfect and
complete, lacking in nothing.
JAMES 1:2–4 NASB

You make known to me the path of life;
you will fill me with joy in your presence,
with eternal pleasures at your right hand.

PSALM 16:11 NIV

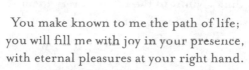

Those who live at the ends of the earth stand in
awe of your wonders. From where the sun rises
to where it sets, you inspire shouts of joy.

PSALM 65:8 NLT

But even if I am being poured out as a drink offering
upon the sacrifice and service of your faith, I rejoice
and share my joy with you all. You too, I urge you,
rejoice in the same way and share your joy with me.

PHILIPPIANS 2:17–18 NASB

"The kingdom of heaven is like a treasure
hidden in the field, which a man found and hid
again; and from joy over it he goes and sells
all that he has and buys that field."

MATTHEW 13:44 NASB

Sing joyfully to the LORD, you righteous;
it is fitting for the upright to praise him.

PSALM 33:1 NIV

What we have seen and heard we proclaim to you
also, so that you too may have fellowship with us;
and indeed our fellowship is with the Father,
and with His Son Jesus Christ. These things we
write, so that our joy may be made complete.

1 JOHN 1:3–4 NASB

I will praise you with the harp for your faithfulness,
my God; I will sing praise to you with the lyre, Holy
One of Israel. My lips will shout for joy when I sing
praise to you—I whom you have delivered.

PSALM 71:22–23 NIV

And though you have not seen Him, you love
Him, and though you do not see Him now,
but believe in Him, you greatly rejoice with joy
inexpressible and full of glory, obtaining as the
outcome of your faith the salvation of your souls.

1 PETER 1:8–9 NASB

Jesus saw that they wanted to ask him about this, so he said to them, "Are you asking one another what I meant when I said, 'In a little while you will see me no more, and then after a little while you will see me'? Very truly I tell you, you will weep and mourn while the world rejoices. You will grieve, but your grief will turn to joy. A woman giving birth to a child has pain because her time has come; but when her baby is born she forgets the anguish because of her joy that a child is born into the world. So with you: Now is your time of grief, but I will see you again and you will rejoice, and no one will take away your joy."

JOHN 16:19–22 NIV

And the disciples were continually filled
with joy and with the Holy Spirit.

ACTS 13:52 NASB

For the kingdom of God is not a matter of
eating and drinking, but of righteousness,
peace and joy in the Holy Spirit.

ROMANS 14:17 NIV

I have no greater joy than this, to hear
of my children walking in the truth.
3 JOHN 1:4 NASB

Oh come, let us sing to the LORD! Let us shout
joyfully to the Rock of our salvation.
PSALM 95:1 NKJV

Tell the heavens and the earth to be glad and
celebrate! Command the ocean to roar with all
of its creatures and the fields to rejoice with all of
their crops. Then every tree in the forest will sing
joyful songs to the LORD. He is coming to judge
all people on earth with fairness and truth.
PSALM 96:11–13 CEV

Now to Him who is able to keep you from
stumbling, and to make you stand in the presence
of His glory blameless with great joy, to the only
God our Savior, through Jesus Christ our Lord,
be glory, majesty, dominion and authority,
before all time and now and forever. Amen.
JUDE 1:24–25 NASB

For you make me glad by your deeds, LORD;
I sing for joy at what your hands have done.
PSALM 92:4 NIV

Rejoice in the Lord always.
I will say it again: Rejoice!
PHILIPPIANS 4:4 NIV

Always be joyful and never stop praying.
Whatever happens, keep thanking God because of
Jesus Christ. This is what God wants you to do.
1 THESSALONIANS 5:16–18 CEV

Then I heard what sounded like a great multitude,
like the roar of rushing waters and like loud peals of
thunder, shouting: "Hallelujah! For our Lord God
Almighty reigns. Let us rejoice and be glad and give
him glory! For the wedding of the Lamb has come,
and his bride has made herself ready.
REVELATION 19:6–7 NIV

Satisfy us in the morning with your unfailing love,
that we may sing for joy and be glad all our days.
PSALM 90:14 NIV

"You yourselves bear me witness, that I said,
'I am not the Christ,' but, 'I have been sent before
Him.' He who has the bride is the bridegroom;
but the friend of the bridegroom, who stands
and hears him, rejoices greatly because of the
bridegroom's voice. Therefore this joy of mine is
fulfilled. He must increase, but I must decrease."
JOHN 3:28–30 NKJV

"I tell you that in the same way, there will
be more joy in heaven over one sinner
who repents than over ninety-nine righteous
persons who need no repentance."
LUKE 15:7 NASB

Light shines on the righteous and
joy on the upright in heart.
PSALM 97:11 NIV

For the LORD takes delight in his people; he crowns
the humble with victory. Let his faithful people
rejoice in this honor and sing for joy on their beds.
PSALM 149:4–5 NIV

Sing to the LORD a new song,
for he has done marvelous things.
PSALM 98:1 NIV

I have inherited Your testimonies forever,
for they are the joy of my heart.
PSALM 119:111 NASB

"For you will go out with joy and be led forth
with peace; the mountains and the hills will
break forth into shouts of joy before you,
and all the trees of the field will clap their hands."
ISAIAH 55:12 NASB

A joyful heart is good medicine,
but a broken spirit dries up the bones.
PROVERBS 17:22 NASB

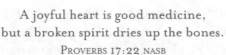

Shout for joy, O heavens! And rejoice, O earth!
Break forth into joyful shouting, O mountains!
For the LORD has comforted His people and
will have compassion on His afflicted.
ISAIAH 49:13 NASB

May those who delight in my vindication shout for
joy and gladness; may they always say, "The LORD be
exalted, who delights in the well-being of his servant."
PSALM 35:27 NIV

I know that there is nothing better for people
than to be happy and to do good while they live.
ECCLESIASTES 3:12 NIV

I Give You Strength

I am your Lord, your supply. You must rely on Me. Trust to the last uttermost limit. Trust and be not afraid. You must depend on divine power only. I have not forgotten you. Your help is coming. You shall know and realize My power.

Endurance is faith tried almost to the breaking point. You must wait and trust and hope and joy in Me. You must not depend on man but on Me—on Me, your Strength, your Help, your Supply.

This is the great test. Am I your supply or not? Every great work for Me has had to have this great test-time.

Possess your souls in patience and rejoice. You must wait until I show the way. Heaven itself cannot contain more joy than that soul knows, when, after the waiting-test, I crown it victor, but no disciple of Mine can be victor who does not wait until I give the order to start. You cannot be anxious if you know that I am your supply.

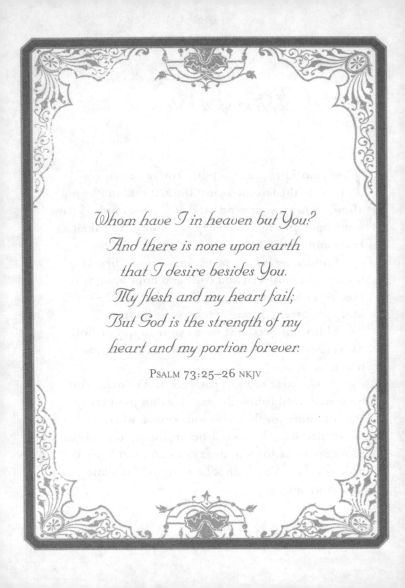

Whom have I in heaven but You?
And there is none upon earth
that I desire besides You.
My flesh and my heart fail;
But God is the strength of my
heart and my portion forever.

PSALM 73:25–26 NKJV

God is our refuge and strength,
an ever-present help in trouble.
PSALM 46:1 NIV

"And in the future, your children will ask you,
'What does all this mean?' Then you will tell them,
'With the power of his mighty hand, the LORD brought
us out of Egypt, the place of our slavery.'"
EXODUS 13:14 NLT

Be thou exalted, LORD, in thine own strength:
so will we sing and praise thy power.
PSALM 21:13 KJV

"God is powerful and dreadful. He enforces peace in
the heavens. Who is able to count his heavenly army?
Doesn't his light shine on all the earth?"
JOB 25:2–3 NLT

You, God, are awesome in your sanctuary;
the God of Israel gives power and strength
to his people. Praise be to God!
PSALM 68:35 NIV

"Yours, O LORD, is the greatness, the power,
the glory, the victory, and the majesty. Everything
in the heavens and on earth is yours, O Lord,
and this is your kingdom. We adore you
as the one who is over all things."

1 CHRONICLES 29:11 NLT

My flesh and my heart may fail, but God is the
strength of my heart and my portion forever.

PSALM 73:26 NIV

"Wealth and honor come from you alone,
for you rule over everything. Power and
might are in your hand, and at your discretion
people are made great and given strength."

1 CHRONICLES 29:12 NLT

"Your right hand, O LORD, is glorious in power.
Your right hand, O LORD, smashes the enemy."

EXODUS 15:6 NLT

God hath spoken once; twice have I heard this;
that power belongeth unto God.
PSALM 62:11 KJV

The voice of the LORD is powerful;
the voice of the LORD is full of majesty.
PSALM 29:4 KJV

But I will sing of thy power; yea, I will sing aloud of
thy mercy in the morning: for thou hast been my
defence and refuge in the day of my trouble.
PSALM 59:16 KJV

"For the Lord GOD will help Me; therefore I
will not be disgraced; therefore I have set My face
like a flint, and I know that I will not be ashamed.
He is near who justifies Me; who will contend with
Me? Let us stand together. Who is My adversary?
Let him come near Me."
ISAIAH 50:7–8 NKJV

He ruleth by his power for ever; his eyes behold the
nations: let not the rebellious exalt themselves. Selah.
PSALM 66:7 KJV

Proclaim the power of God, whose majesty is over
Israel, whose power is in the heavens. You, God,
are awesome in your sanctuary; the God of Israel
gives power and strength to his people.
Praise be to God!
PSALM 68:34–35 NIV

For the foolishness of God is wiser than
human wisdom, and the weakness of God
is stronger than human strength.
I CORINTHIANS 1:25 NIV

Man did eat angels' food: he sent them meat to the
full. He caused an east wind to blow in the heaven:
and by his power he brought in the south wind.
PSALM 78:25–26 KJV

The LORD replied, "Listen, I am making a covenant
with you in the presence of all your people. I will
perform miracles that have never been performed
anywhere in all the earth or in any nation. And all the
people around you will see the power of the LORD—
the awesome power I will display for you."
EXODUS 34:10 NLT

Great is our Lord, and of great power:
his understanding is infinite.
PSALM 147:5 KJV

All thy works shall praise thee,
O LORD; and thy saints shall bless thee.
They shall speak of the glory of
thy kingdom, and talk of thy power;
to make known to the sons of men his mighty acts,
and the glorious majesty of his kingdom.
PSALM 145:10–12 KJV

May the Lord make your love increase and
overflow for each other and for everyone else,
just as ours does for you. May he strengthen
your hearts so that you will be blameless and
holy in the presence of our God and Father when
our Lord Jesus comes with all his holy ones.

1 THESSALONIANS 3:12–13 NIV

If anyone speaks, they should do so as one who speaks
the very words of God. If anyone serves, they should
do so with the strength God provides, so that in all
things God may be praised through Jesus Christ.
To him be the glory and the power
for ever and ever. Amen.

1 PETER 4:11 NIV

Lift up your eyes on high and see who has created
these stars, the One who leads forth their host
by number, He calls them all by name; because
of the greatness of His might and the strength
of His power, not one of them is missing.

ISAIAH 40:26 NASB

"The LORD is my strength and my defense;
he has become my salvation. He is my God,
and I will praise him, my father's God,
and I will exalt him."
EXODUS 15:2 NIV

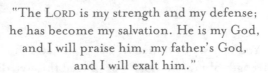

But our citizenship is in heaven. And we eagerly
await a Savior from there, the Lord Jesus Christ, who,
by the power that enables him to bring everything
under his control, will transform our lowly bodies
so that they will be like his glorious body.
PHILIPPIANS 3:20–21 NIV

It is He who made the earth by His power,
who established the world by His wisdom;
and by His understanding He has
stretched out the heavens.
JEREMIAH 10:12 NASB

If he holds back the rain, the earth becomes a
desert. If he releases the waters, they flood the earth.
Yes, strength and wisdom are his; deceivers and
deceived are both in his power.
JOB 12:15–16 NLT

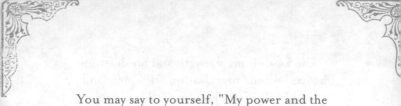

You may say to yourself, "My power and the strength of my hands have produced this wealth for me." But remember the LORD your God, for it is he who gives you the ability to produce wealth, and so confirms his covenant, which he swore to your ancestors, as it is today.

DEUTERONOMY 8:17–18 NIV

"God, in his power, drags away the rich. They may rise high, but they have no assurance of life."

JOB 24:22 NLT

"Ah Lord GOD! Behold, You have made the heavens and the earth by Your great power and by Your outstretched arm! Nothing is too difficult for You."

JEREMIAH 32:17 NASB

"When I raise my powerful hand and bring out the Israelites, the Egyptians will know that I am the LORD."

EXODUS 7:5 NLT

"But true wisdom and power are found in God;
counsel and understanding are his."
JOB 12:13 NLT

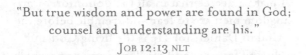

He came to His hometown and began teaching them
in their synagogue, so that they were astonished, and
said, "Where did this man get this wisdom and these
miraculous powers? Is not this the carpenter's son?
Is not His mother called Mary, and His brothers,
James and Joseph and Simon and Judas?"
MATTHEW 13:54–55 NASB

The angel answered, The Holy Spirit will come
upon you, the power of the Highest hover
over you; therefore, the child you bring to
birth will be called Holy, Son of God.
LUKE 1:35 MSG

And my God shall supply all your need
according to His riches in glory by Christ Jesus.
PHILIPPIANS 4:19 NKJV

"I make a decree that in all the dominion of my kingdom men are to fear and tremble before the God of Daniel; for He is the living God and enduring forever, and His kingdom is one which will not be destroyed, and His dominion will be forever. He delivers and rescues and performs signs and wonders in heaven and on earth, who has also delivered Daniel from the power of the lions."

DANIEL 6:26–27 NASB

The LORD is slow to anger and great in power, and the LORD will by no means leave the guilty unpunished. In whirlwind and storm is His way, and clouds are the dust beneath His feet.

NAHUM 1:3 NASB

"Now may the Lord's strength be displayed, just as you have declared: 'The LORD is slow to anger, abounding in love and forgiving sin and rebellion. Yet he does not leave the guilty unpunished; he punishes the children for the sin of the parents to the third and fourth generation.'"

NUMBERS 14:17–18 NIV

I Will Give You Rest

Never doubt. Have no fear. Watch the faintest tremor of fear, and stop all work, everything, and rest before Me until you are joyful and strong again.

Deal in the same way with all tired feelings. I was weary too, when on earth, and I separated Myself from My disciples and sat and rested on the well. Rested—and then it was that the Samaritan woman was helped.

I had to teach renewal of Spirit—force rest of body to My disciples. Then, as your example, I lay with My head on a pillow, asleep in the boat. It was not, as they thought, indifference. They cried, "Master, carest thou not that we perish?" and I had to teach them that ceaseless activity was no part of My Father's plan.

When Paul said, "I can do all things through Christ which strengtheneth me," he did not mean that he was to do all things and then rely on Me to find strength. He meant that for all I told him to do, he could rely on My supplying the strength.

My work in the world has been hindered by work, work, work. Many a tireless, nervous body has driven a spirit. The spirit should be the master always and just simply and naturally use the body as need should arise. Rest in Me.

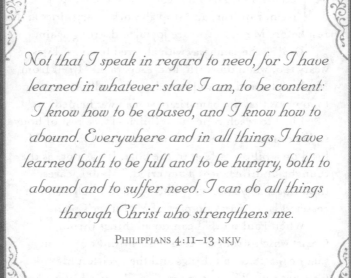

Not that I speak in regard to need, for I have learned in whatever state I am, to be content: I know how to be abased, and I know how to abound. Everywhere and in all things I have learned both to be full and to be hungry, both to abound and to suffer need. I can do all things through Christ who strengthens me.

PHILIPPIANS 4:11–13 NKJV

Do not be anxious about anything, but in every
situation, by prayer and petition, with thanksgiving,
present your requests to God. And the peace of
God, which transcends all understanding, will guard
your hearts and your minds in Christ Jesus.

PHILIPPIANS 4:6–7 NIV

And suddenly a great tempest arose
on the sea, so that the boat was covered
with the waves. But He was asleep.

MATTHEW 8:24 NKJV

Then he returned to the disciples and said
to them, "Are you still sleeping and resting?
Look, the hour has come, and the Son of
Man is delivered into the hands of sinners."

MATTHEW 26:45 NIV

This is what the LORD says:
"Stop at the crossroads and look around.
Ask for the old, godly way, and walk in it.
Travel its path, and you will find rest for your souls."

JEREMIAH 6:16 NLT

I have told you this, so that you might have
peace in your hearts because of me. While
you are in the world, you will have to suffer.
But cheer up! I have defeated the world.
JOHN 16:33 CEV

And on the seventh day God ended His work
which He had done, and He rested on the seventh
day from all His work which He had done.
GENESIS 2:2 NKJV

Do you not know? Have you not heard? The LORD
is the everlasting God, the Creator of the ends
of the earth. He will not grow tired or weary,
and his understanding no one can fathom.
ISAIAH 40:28 NIV

For God alone, O my soul, wait in silence,
for my hope is from him.
PSALM 62:5 ESV

Be still before the LORD and wait patiently for him;
do not fret when people succeed in their ways,
when they carry out their wicked schemes.
PSALM 37:7 NIV

It is in vain that you rise up early and go
late to rest, eating the bread of anxious toil;
for he gives to his beloved sleep.
PSALM 127:2 ESV

My soul is weary with sorrow;
strengthen me according to your word.
PSALM 119:28 NIV

"I will feed My flock and I will lead them to rest,"
declares the Lord GOD.
EZEKIEL 34:15 NASB

When you lie down, you will not be afraid;
when you lie down, your sleep will be sweet.
PROVERBS 3:24 NIV

"Peace I leave with you; my peace I give you.
I do not give to you as the world gives. Do not
let your hearts be troubled and do not be afraid."
JOHN 14:27 NIV

May integrity and uprightness
preserve me, for I wait for you.
PSALM 25:21 ESV

The LORD replied, "My Presence
will go with you, and I will give you rest."
EXODUS 33:14 NIV

Then God blessed the seventh day and
sanctified it, because in it He rested from all
His work which God had created and made.

GENESIS 2:3 NKJV

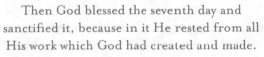

Dear children, let us not love with words or
speech but with actions and in truth. This is
how we know that we belong to the truth and how
we set our hearts at rest in his presence: If our
hearts condemn us, we know that God is greater
than our hearts, and he knows everything.

1 JOHN 3:18–20 NIV

"Come to Me, all who are weary and heavy-laden,
and I will give you rest. Take My yoke upon you and
learn from Me, for I am gentle and humble in heart,
and you will find rest for your souls."

MATTHEW 11:28–29 NASB

You are my mighty rock, my fortress,
my protector, the rock where I am safe, my shield,
my powerful weapon, and my place of shelter.

PSALM 18:2 CEV

The apostles gathered around Jesus and reported
to him all they had done and taught. Then,
because so many people were coming and going
that they did not even have a chance to eat, he said
to them, "Come with me by yourselves to a quiet
place and get some rest." So they went away by
themselves in a boat to a solitary place.

MARK 6:30–32 NIV

The fear of the LORD leads to life;
then one rests content, untouched by trouble.

PROVERBS 19:23 NIV

Rest in the LORD and wait patiently for Him;
do not fret because of him who prospers in his way,
because of the man who carries out wicked schemes.

PSALM 37:7 NASB

He restores my soul; He guides me in the
paths of righteousness for His name's sake.

PSALM 23:3 NASB

On God my salvation and my glory rest;
the rock of my strength, my refuge is in God.
PSALM 62:7 NASB

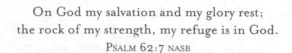

"Six days you shall do your work, and on the
seventh day you shall rest, that your ox and your
donkey may rest, and the son of your female
servant and the stranger may be refreshed."
EXODUS 23:12 NKJV

The law of the LORD is perfect,
restoring the soul; the testimony of the
LORD is sure, making wise the simple.
PSALM 19:7 NASB

"I will refresh the weary and satisfy the faint."
JEREMIAH 31:25 NIV

It is good that one should hope and
wait quietly for the salvation of the LORD.
LAMENTATIONS 3:26 NKJV

Comfort, comfort my people, says your God.
ISAIAH 40:1 ESV

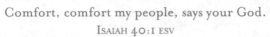

Praise be to the God and Father of our Lord
Jesus Christ, the Father of compassion and the God
of all comfort, who comforts us in all our troubles,
so that we can comfort those in any trouble with
the comfort we ourselves receive from God.
2 CORINTHIANS 1:3–4 NIV

Showing respect to the LORD brings true life—
if you do it, you can relax without fear of danger.
PROVERBS 19:23 CEV

The wolf will live with the lamb, the leopard will lie
down with the goat, the calf and the lion and the
yearling together; and a little child will lead them.
ISAIAH 11:6 NIV

He says, "Be still, and know that I am God;
I will be exalted among the nations,
I will be exalted in the earth."
PSALM 46:10 NIV

He who dwells in the secret place of the Most High
shall abide under the shadow of the Almighty.
PSALM 91:1 NKJV

"The LORD will fight for you;
you need only to be still."
EXODUS 14:14 NIV

Then He arose and rebuked the wind,
and said to the sea, "Peace, be still!" And
the wind ceased and there was a great calm.
MARK 4:39 NKJV

For in six days the LORD made the heavens
and the earth, the sea, and all that is in them,
and rested the seventh day. Therefore the LORD
blessed the Sabbath day and hallowed it.

EXODUS 20:11 NKJV

Then times of refreshment will come from the
presence of the Lord, and he will again send
you Jesus, your appointed Messiah. For he must
remain in heaven until the time for the final
restoration of all things, as God promised
long ago through his holy prophets.

ACTS 3:20–21 NLT

Do not do any work on that day, because it
is the Day of Atonement, when atonement
is made for you before the LORD your God.

LEVITICUS 23:28 NIV

And God will provide rest for you who are
being persecuted and also for us when the
Lord Jesus appears from heaven.

2 THESSALONIANS 1:7 NLT

I Will Hear You

I will be much entreated because I know that only in that earnest supplication, and the calm trust that results, does man learn strength and gain peace. Therefore I have laid that incessant, persistent pleading as a duty upon My disciples.

Never weary in prayer. When one day man sees how marvelously his prayer has been answered, then he will deeply, so deeply, regret that he prayed so little.

Prayer changes all. Prayer re-creates. Prayer is irresistible. So pray, literally without ceasing.

Pray until you almost cease to pray, because trust has become so rocklike, and then pray on because it has become so much a habit that you cannot resist it.

And always pray until prayer merges into praise. That is the only note on which true prayer should end. It is the love and laughter of your attitude toward man interpreted in the prayer and praise of your attitude toward God.

Confess your trespasses to one another,
and pray for one another, that you may
be healed. The effective, fervent prayer
of a righteous man avails much.

JAMES 5:16 NKJV

Seek the LORD while you can find him.
Call on him now while he is near.
ISAIAH 55:6 NLT

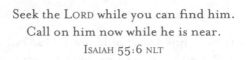

For this reason, ever since I heard about your faith in
the Lord Jesus and your love for all God's people, I have
not stopped giving thanks for you, remembering you in
my prayers. I keep asking that the God of our Lord Jesus
Christ, the glorious Father, may give you the Spirit of
wisdom and revelation, so that you may know him better.
EPHESIANS 1:15–17 NIV

Rejoice always, pray continually,
give thanks in all circumstances; for this
is God's will for you in Christ Jesus.
1 THESSALONIANS 5:16–18 NIV

But I cry to you for help, LORD;
in the morning my prayer comes before you.
PSALM 88:13 NIV

Answer me when I call, O God of my
righteousness! You have relieved me in my
distress; be gracious to me and hear my prayer.
PSALM 4:1 NASB

"This, then, is how you should pray: 'Our Father in heaven, hallowed be your name, your kingdom come, your will be done, on earth as it is in heaven. Give us today our daily bread. And forgive us our debts, as we also have forgiven our debtors. And lead us not into temptation, but deliver us from the evil one.'"

MATTHEW 6:9–13 NIV

Pray to me in time of trouble.
I will rescue you, and you will honor me.

PSALM 50:15 CEV

If anyone sees his brother committing a sin not leading to death, he shall ask and God will for him give life to those who commit sin not leading to death. There is a sin leading to death; I do not say that he should make request for this.

1 JOHN 5:16 NASB

Pray for us, for we are sure that we have a good conscience, desiring to conduct ourselves honorably in all things.

HEBREWS 13:18 NASB

I thank my God every time I remember you.
In all my prayers for all of you, I always pray with
joy because of your partnership in the gospel from
the first day until now, being confident of this,
that he who began a good work in you will carry it
on to completion until the day of Christ Jesus.

PHILIPPIANS 1:3–6 NIV

I patiently waited, LORD, for you to hear my prayer.
You listened and pulled me from a lonely pit full
of mud and mire. You let me stand on a rock with
my feet firm, and you gave me a new song, a song of
praise to you. Many will see this, and they will
honor and trust you, the LORD God.

PSALM 40:1–3 CEV

The LORD is near to all who call upon Him,
to all who call upon Him in truth.

PSALM 145:18 NASB

Devote yourselves to prayer,
being watchful and thankful.
COLOSSIANS 4:2 NIV

When his people pray for help,
he listens and rescues them from their troubles.
PSALM 34:17 CEV

If you declare with your mouth, "Jesus is Lord,"
and believe in your heart that God raised him from
the dead, you will be saved. For it is with your heart
that you believe and are justified, and it is with your
mouth that you profess your faith and are saved.
ROMANS 10:9–10 NIV

If we claim to be without sin, we deceive ourselves
and the truth is not in us. If we confess our sins,
he is faithful and just and will forgive us our sins
and purify us from all unrighteousness. If we
claim we have not sinned, we make him out
to be a liar and his word is not in us.
1 JOHN 1:8–10 NIV

Do not be anxious about anything, but in
every situation, by prayer and petition, with
thanksgiving, present your requests to God.
PHILIPPIANS 4:6 NIV

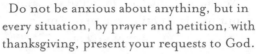

In the same way the Spirit also helps our weakness;
for we do not know how to pray as we should, but the
Spirit Himself intercedes for us with groanings too
deep for words; and He who searches the hearts knows
what the mind of the Spirit is, because He intercedes
for the saints according to the will of God.
ROMANS 8:26–27 NASB

Heed the sound of my cry for help,
my King and my God, for to You I pray.
PSALM 5:2 NASB

Never stop praying, especially for others.
Always pray by the power of the Spirit.
Stay alert and keep praying for God's people.
EPHESIANS 6:18 CEV

We always thank God for all of you and
continually mention you in our prayers.
1 Thessalonians 1:2 niv

His father was sick in bed, suffering from fever
and dysentery. Paul went in to see him and, after
prayer, placed his hands on him and healed him.
Acts 28:8 niv

In those days Hezekiah became mortally ill;
and he prayed to the Lord, and the Lord
spoke to him and gave him a sign.
2 Chronicles 32:24 nasb

Please listen to my prayer and my cry for help,
as I lift my hands toward your holy temple.
Psalm 28:2 cev

I prayed to you, Lord God, and you healed me,
saving me from death and the grave.
Psalm 30:2–3 cev

But when you pray, go into your room, close the door
and pray to your Father, who is unseen. Then your
Father, who sees what is done in secret, will reward
you. And when you pray, do not keep on babbling
like pagans, for they think they will be heard because
of their many words. Do not be like them, for your
Father knows what you need before you ask him.

MATTHEW 6:6–8 NIV

David built there an altar to the LORD and
offered burnt offerings and peace offerings.
Thus the Lord was moved by prayer for the land,
and the plague was held back from Israel.

2 SAMUEL 24:25 NASB

And when he had taken it, the four living
creatures and the twenty-four elders fell down
before the Lamb. Each one had a harp and they
were holding golden bowls full of incense,
which are the prayers of God's people.

REVELATION 5:8 NIV

"Therefore I tell you, whatever you ask for in prayer,
believe that you have received it, and it will be yours."

MARK 11:24 NIV

During the days of Jesus' life on earth, he offered up
prayers and petitions with fervent cries and tears to
the one who could save him from death, and he was
heard because of his reverent submission.

HEBREWS 5:7 NIV

She, greatly distressed, prayed to
the LORD and wept bitterly.

1 SAMUEL 1:10 NASB

"For the eyes of the Lord are on the righteous
and his ears are attentive to their prayer,
but the face of the Lord is against those who do evil."

1 PETER 3:12 NIV

Is anyone among you in trouble? Let them pray.
Is anyone happy? Let them sing songs of praise.
JAMES 5:13 NIV

The people therefore cried out to Moses, and
Moses prayed to the LORD and the fire died out.
NUMBERS 11:2 NASB

The smoke of the incense, together with the
prayers of God's people, went up before
God from the angel's hand.
REVELATION 8:4 NIV

"Now therefore, I pray You, if I have found favor
in Your sight, let me know Your ways that I may
know You, so that I may find favor in Your sight.
Consider too, that this nation is Your people."
EXODUS 33:13 NASB

So I turned to the Lord God and pleaded
with him in prayer and petition, in fasting,
and in sackcloth and ashes.
DANIEL 9:3 NIV

My Plans Are Perfect

C hildren, take every moment as of My planning and ordering. Remember your Master is the Lord of the day's little happenings. In all the small things yield to My gentle pressure on your arm. Stay or go, as that pressure, Love's pressure, indicates. The Lord of the moments, Creator of the snowdrop and the mighty oak. More tender with the snowdrop than the oak.

And when things do not fall out according to your plan, then smile at Me indulgently, a smile of love, and say, as you would to a human loved one, "Have Your way then"—knowing that My loving response will be to make that way as easy for your feet as it can be.

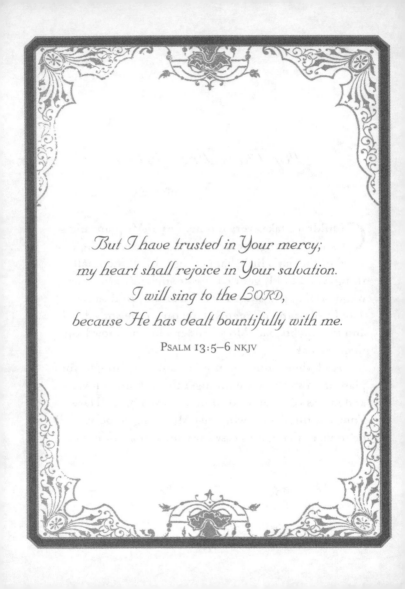

But I have trusted in Your mercy;
my heart shall rejoice in Your salvation.
I will sing to the LORD,
because He has dealt bountifully with me.

PSALM 13:5–6 NKJV

Be thankful in all circumstances, for this is
God's will for you who belong to Christ Jesus.
1 Thessalonians 5:18 nlt

For it is God's will that by doing good you
should silence the ignorant talk of foolish people.
1 Peter 2:15 niv

For it is better, if it is God's will,
to suffer for doing good than for doing evil.
1 Peter 3:17 niv

For you know what instructions we gave you by
the authority of the Lord Jesus. It is God's will
that you should be sanctified: that you should avoid
sexual immorality; that each of you should learn
to control your own body in a way that is holy and
honorable, not in passionate lust like the
pagans, who do not know God.
1 Thessalonians 4:2–5 niv

So then, those who suffer according to God's
will should commit themselves to their faithful
Creator and continue to do good.

1 PETER 4:19 NIV

For the gospel has for this purpose been preached
even to those who are dead, that though they are
judged in the flesh as men, they may live in
the spirit according to the will of God.

1 PETER 4:6 NASB

Jesus answered, "My teaching is not my own.
It comes from the one who sent me. Anyone who
chooses to do the will of God will find out whether
my teaching comes from God or whether I speak
on my own. Whoever speaks on their own does so
to gain personal glory, but he who seeks the glory
of the one who sent him is a man of truth;
there is nothing false about him."

JOHN 7:16–18 NIV

So do not throw away your confidence; it will
be richly rewarded. You need to persevere so that
when you have done the will of God, you will receive
what he has promised. For, "In just a little while,
he who is coming will come and will not delay."

 HEBREWS 10:35–37 NIV

And do not be conformed to this world,
but be transformed by the renewing of your
mind, that you may prove what is that good
and acceptable and perfect will of God.

ROMANS 12:2 NKJV

"For My thoughts are not your thoughts, nor are your
ways My ways," says the LORD. "For as the heavens are
higher than the earth, so are My ways higher than your
ways, and My thoughts than your thoughts."

ISAIAH 55:8–9 NKJV

The world is passing away, and also its lusts;
but the one who does the will of God lives forever.

I JOHN 2:17 NASB

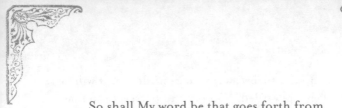

So shall My word be that goes forth from
My mouth; it shall not return to Me void,
but it shall accomplish what I please, and it
shall prosper in the thing for which I sent it.

ISAIAH 55:11 NKJV

They replied, "We want to perform God's
works, too. What should we do?" Jesus told
them, "This is the only work God wants from
you: Believe in the one he has sent."

JOHN 6:28–29 NLT

"For I know the plans I have for you," says the LORD.
"They are plans for good and not for disaster,
to give you a future and a hope."

JEREMIAH 29:11 NLT

"Ask me and I will tell you remarkable secrets
you do not know about things to come."

JEREMIAH 33:3 NLT

"I am the LORD, who opened a way through the waters,
making a dry path through the sea. I called forth the
mighty army of Egypt with all its chariots and horses.
I drew them beneath the waves, and they drowned,
their lives snuffed out like a smoldering candlewick.
"But forget all that—it is nothing compared to what
I am going to do. For I am about to do something
new. See, I have already begun! Do you not see it?
I will make a pathway through the wilderness.
I will create rivers in the dry wasteland."

ISAIAH 43:16–19 NLT

The sinful nature wants to do evil, which is just
the opposite of what the Spirit wants. And the
Spirit gives us desires that are the opposite of what
the sinful nature desires. These two forces are
constantly fighting each other, so you are not
free to carry out your good intentions.

GALATIANS 5:17 NLT

So be careful how you live. Don't live like fools,
but like those who are wise. Make the most of every
opportunity in these evil days. Don't act thoughtlessly,
but understand what the Lord wants you to do.

EPHESIANS 5:15–17 NLT

Jesus came and told his disciples, "I have been given
all authority in heaven and on earth. Therefore,
go and make disciples of all the nations, baptizing
them in the name of the Father and the Son and the
Holy Spirit. Teach these new disciples to obey all the
commands I have given you. And be sure of this:
I am with you always, even to the end of the age."

MATTHEW 28:18–20 NLT

The Lord isn't really being slow about his promise,
as some people think. No, he is being patient for
your sake. He does not want anyone to be destroyed,
but wants everyone to repent.

2 PETER 3:9 NLT

And I know that whatever God does is final.
Nothing can be added to it or taken from it.
God's purpose is that people should fear him.

ECCLESIASTES 3:14 NLT

Commit your works to the LORD
and your plans will be established.
The LORD has made everything for its own purpose,
even the wicked for the day of evil.

PROVERBS 16:3–4 NASB

I alone am God!
There are no other gods; no one is like me.
Think about what happened many years ago.
From the very beginning, I told what
would happen long before it took place.

ISAIAH 46:9–10 CEV

God's purpose was that we Jews who were the first to trust in Christ would bring praise and glory to God. And now you Gentiles have also heard the truth, the Good News that God saves you. And when you believed in Christ, he identified you as his own by giving you the Holy Spirit, whom he promised long ago.

EPHESIANS 1:12–13 NLT

When all the people and the tax collectors heard this, they acknowledged God's justice, having been baptized with the baptism of John. But the Pharisees and the lawyers rejected God's purpose for themselves, not having been baptized by John.

LUKE 7:29–30 NASB

But have nothing to do with worldly fables fit only for old women. On the other hand, discipline yourself for the purpose of godliness; for bodily discipline is only of little profit, but godliness is profitable for all things, since it holds promise for the present life and also for the life to come.

1 TIMOTHY 4:7–8 NASB

The LORD foils the plans of the nations;
he thwarts the purposes of the peoples.
But the plans of the LORD stand firm forever,
the purposes of his heart through all generations.

PSALM 33:10–11 NIV

Now the one who has fashioned us for this very
purpose is God, who has given us the Spirit as a
deposit, guaranteeing what is to come. Therefore we
are always confident and know that as long as we are at
home in the body we are away from the Lord.

2 CORINTHIANS 5:5–6 NIV

"I desire to do your will, my God;
your law is within my heart."

PSALM 40:8 NIV

The LORD will guide you always; he will satisfy your
needs in a sun-scorched land and will strengthen
your frame. You will be like a well-watered garden,
like a spring whose waters never fail.

ISAIAH 58:11 NIV

Your eyes saw my unformed body; all the days
ordained for me were written in your book
before one of them came to be.

PSALM 139:16 NIV

For God so loved the world that he gave his one
and only Son, that whoever believes in him shall
not perish but have eternal life. For God did not
send his Son into the world to condemn the world,
but to save the world through him.

JOHN 3:16–17 NIV

"Therefore, I testify to you this day that I am innocent
of the blood of all men. For I did not shrink from
declaring to you the whole purpose of God."

ACTS 20:26–27 NASB

My Power Is Limitless

Is My hand shortened that it cannot save? No! My power to save increases as your power to understand My salvation increases. So from strength to strength, from power to power, we go in union.

Limitless is My miracle-working power in the universe, though it has limitations in each individual life, but only to the extent of the lack of vision of that individual. There is no limit to My power to save. Also there is no limit to My desire and longing to save. My hand is not shortened, and it is "stretched out still," longing and waiting to be allowed to bless and help and save.

Think how tenderly I respect the right of each individual soul. Never forcing upon it My help, My salvation. Perhaps in all My suffering for humanity, that is the hardest, the restraint of the divine impatience and longing to help, until the call of the soul gives Me My right to act.

Think of love shown in this. Comfort My waiting, loving, longing heart by claiming My help, guidance, and miracle-working power.

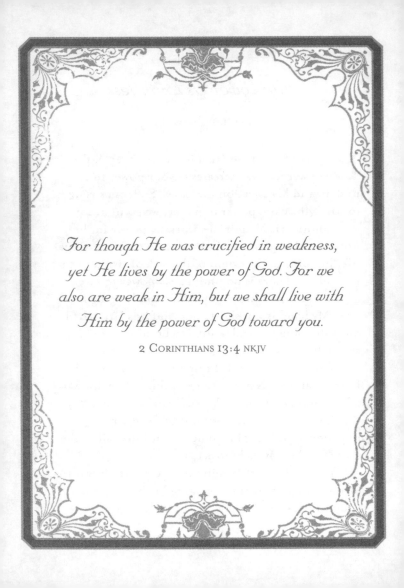

For though He was crucified in weakness,
yet He lives by the power of God. For we
also are weak in Him, but we shall live with
Him by the power of God toward you.

2 CORINTHIANS 13:4 NKJV

But God made the earth by his power, and
he preserves it by his wisdom. With his own
understanding he stretched out the heavens.
JEREMIAH 10:12 NLT

"But indeed for this purpose I have raised you up,
that I may show My power in you, and that My
name may be declared in all the earth."
EXODUS 9:16 NKJV

For by his great power he rules forever.
He watches every movement of the nations;
let no rebel rise in defiance.
PSALM 66:7 NLT

"Your right hand, O LORD, has become glorious in
power; Your right hand, O LORD, has dashed the enemy
in pieces. And in the greatness of Your excellence You
have overthrown those who rose against You."
EXODUS 15:6–7 NKJV

For to be sure, he was crucified in weakness,
yet he lives by God's power. Likewise, we are
weak in him, yet by God's power we will live
with him in our dealing with you.
2 CORINTHIANS 13:4 NIV

One thing God has spoken, two things I have heard:
"Power belongs to you, God, and with you, Lord,
is unfailing love"; and, "You reward everyone
according to what they have done."
PSALM 62:11–12 NIV

The voice of the LORD echoes above the sea.
The God of glory thunders.
The LORD thunders over the mighty sea.
PSALM 29:3 NLT

To Him who rides on the heaven
of heavens, which were of old! Indeed,
He sends out His voice, a mighty voice.
PSALM 68:33 NKJV

You have a strong arm; Your hand is mighty,
Your right hand is exalted.
PSALM 89:13 NASB

To him who struck down the firstborn of Egypt
His love endures forever.
and brought Israel out from among them
His love endures forever.
with a mighty hand and outstretched arm.
His love endures forever.
PSALM 136:10–12 NIV

The LORD has bared His holy arm
in the sight of all the nations,
that all the ends of the earth may see
the salvation of our God.
ISAIAH 52:10 NASB

The LORD is slow to anger and great in power,
and the LORD will by no means leave the guilty
unpunished. In whirlwind and storm is His way,
and clouds are the dust beneath His feet.
NAHUM 1:3 NASB

For since the creation of the world His invisible
attributes, His eternal power and divine nature,
have been clearly seen, being understood through
what has been made, so that they are without excuse.

ROMANS 1:20 NASB

A final word: Be strong in the
Lord and in his mighty power.

EPHESIANS 6:10 NLT

Does not the potter have power over the clay,
from the same lump to make one vessel for
honor and another for dishonor?

ROMANS 9:21 NKJV

"Now see that I, even I, am He,
and there is no God besides Me;
I kill and I make alive;
I wound and I heal;
nor is there any who can deliver from My hand."

DEUTERONOMY 32:39 NKJV

He does great things too marvelous to understand.
He performs countless miracles.
JOB 5:9 NLT

"Is anything too hard for the LORD? I will return
about this time next year, and Sarah will have a son."
GENESIS 18:14 NLT

Trust in the LORD always,
for the LORD GOD is the eternal Rock.
ISAIAH 26:4 NLT

All the inhabitants of the earth are reputed as nothing;
He does according to His will in the army of heaven
and among the inhabitants of the earth.
No one can restrain His hand
or say to Him, "What have You done?"
DANIEL 4:35 NKJV

"Who is like you among the gods, O LORD—
glorious in holiness, awesome in splendor,
performing great wonders? You raised your right
hand, and the earth swallowed our enemies."

EXODUS 15:11–12 NLT

The message of the cross is foolish to those who
are headed for destruction! But we who are being
saved know it is the very power of God.

1 CORINTHIANS 1:18 NLT

For I am not ashamed of this Good News about
Christ. It is the power of God at work, saving everyone
who believes—the Jew first and also the Gentile.

ROMANS 1:16 NLT

Then I heard all beings in heaven and on the earth
and under the earth and in the sea offer praise.
Together, all of them were saying, "Praise, honor,
glory, and strength forever and ever to the one
who sits on the throne and to the Lamb!"

REVELATION 5:13 CEV

Finally, let the mighty strength
of the Lord make you strong.
EPHESIANS 6:10 CEV

But you, LORD, are a mighty soldier, standing at my
side. Those troublemakers will fall down and fail—
terribly embarrassed, forever ashamed.
JEREMIAH 20:11 CEV

Finally, my brethren, be strong in the Lord,
and in the power of his might.
EPHESIANS 6:10 KJV

The LORD is my strength, the reason for my song,
because he has saved me. I praise and honor the
LORD—he is my God and the God of my ancestors.
EXODUS 15:2 CEV

Christ gives me the strength to face anything.
PHILIPPIANS 4:13 CEV

That your faith should not stand in the
wisdom of men, but in the power of God.

ɪ Corinthians 2:5 KJV

"Our Lord and God, you are worthy to receive glory,
honor, and power. You created all things, and by
your decision they are and were created."

Revelation 4:11 CEV

Blessed be the God and Father of our Lord Jesus
Christ, which according to his abundant mercy
hath begotten us again unto a lively hope by the
resurrection of Jesus Christ from the dead, to an
inheritance incorruptible, and undefiled, and that
fadeth not away, reserved in heaven for you, who
are kept by the power of God through faith unto
salvation ready to be revealed in the last time.

ɪ Peter 1:3–5 KJV

So Jesus answered and said to them, "Assuredly,
I say to you, if you have faith and do not doubt,
you will not only do what was done to the fig tree,
but also if you say to this mountain, 'Be removed
and be cast into the sea,' it will be done."

MATTHEW 21:21 NKJV

"Have I not commanded you? Be strong
and courageous. Do not be afraid; do not
be discouraged, for the LORD your God
will be with you wherever you go."

JOSHUA 1:9 NIV

The LORD is my light and my salvation—
whom shall I fear?
The LORD is the stronghold of my life—
of whom shall I be afraid?

PSALM 27:1 NIV

Jesus answered, "Why are you afraid? You don't have enough faith." Then Jesus got up and gave a command to the wind and the waves, and it became completely calm. The men were amazed and said, "What kind of man is this? Even the wind and the waves obey him!"

MATTHEW 8:26–27 NCV

Now these are thy servants and thy people, whom thou hast redeemed by thy great power, and by thy strong hand.

NEHEMIAH 1:10 KJV

"Then will appear the sign of the Son of Man in heaven. And then all the peoples of the earth will mourn when they see the Son of Man coming on the clouds of heaven, with power and great glory."

MATTHEW 24:30 NIV

What Jesus did here in Cana of Galilee was the first of the signs through which he revealed his glory; and his disciples believed in him.

JOHN 2:11 NIV

You Are Mine

Rejoice in the fact that you are Mine. The privileges of the members of My kingdom are many. When I said of My Father, "He maketh His sun to rise on the evil and on the good, and sendeth rain on the just and on the unjust," you will notice it was of temporal and material blessings I spoke.

I did not mean that believer and unbeliever could be treated alike. That is not possible; I can send rain and sunshine and money and worldly blessings equally to both, but of the blessing of the kingdom that would be impossible.

There are conditions that control the bestowal of these. My followers do not always understand this, and it is necessary they should do so if they are remembering My injunction which followed—"Be ye therefore perfect even as your Father in heaven is perfect."

To attempt to bestow on all alike your love and understanding and interchange of thought would be impossible. But temporal blessings you, too, bestow, as does My Father. All must be done in love and in the spirit of true forgiveness.

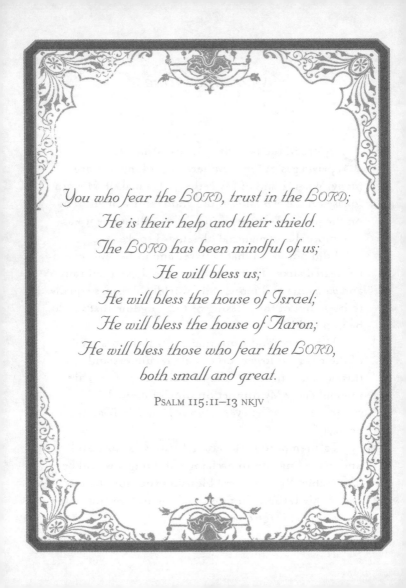

You who fear the LORD, trust in the LORD;

He is their help and their shield.

The LORD has been mindful of us;

He will bless us;

He will bless the house of Israel;

He will bless the house of Aaron;

He will bless those who fear the LORD,

both small and great.

PSALM 115:11–13 NKJV

But to all who did accept him and believe in him
he gave the right to become children of God.

JOHN 1:12 NCV

The Lord isn't slow about keeping his
promises, as some people think he is.
In fact, God is patient, because he wants
everyone to turn from sin and no one to be lost.

2 PETER 3:9 CEV

And when you were baptized, it was the same as
being buried with Christ. Then you were raised
to life because you had faith in the power of
God, who raised Christ from death.

COLOSSIANS 2:12 CEV

"Do not let your hearts be troubled. You believe in
God; believe also in me. My Father's house has many
rooms; if that were not so, would I have told you that
I am going there to prepare a place for you? And if I
go and prepare a place for you, I will come back and
take you to be with me that you also may be where I
am. You know the way to the place where I am going."

JOHN 14:1–4 NIV

Whoever believes and is baptized will be saved,
but whoever does not believe will be condemned.

MARK 16:16 ESV

For he chose us in him before the creation of the
world to be holy and blameless in his sight. In love
he predestined us for adoption to sonship through
Jesus Christ, in accordance with his pleasure and
will—to the praise of his glorious grace, which he
has freely given us in the One he loves.

EPHESIANS 1:4–6 NIV

But those who will be worthy to be raised from the
dead and live again will not marry, nor will they be
given to someone to marry. In that life they are like
angels and cannot die. They are children of God,
because they have been raised from the dead.

LUKE 20:35–36 NCV

Blessed are the peacemakers,
for they will be called children of God.

MATTHEW 5:9 NIV

And you also were included in Christ when you heard the message of truth, the gospel of your salvation. When you believed, you were marked in him with a seal, the promised Holy Spirit, who is a deposit guaranteeing our inheritance until the redemption of those who are God's possession—to the praise of his glory.

EPHESIANS 1:13–14 NIV

Those who are God's children do not continue sinning, because the new life from God remains in them. They are not able to go on sinning, because they have become children of God.

1 JOHN 3:9 NCV

Dear friends, now we are children of God, and we have not yet been shown what we will be in the future. But we know that when Christ comes again, we will be like him, because we will see him as he really is.

1 JOHN 3:2 NCV

But our citizenship is in heaven. And we eagerly await a Savior from there, the Lord Jesus Christ.

PHILIPPIANS 3:20 NIV

But when the set time had fully come, God sent his Son, born of a woman, born under the law, to redeem those under the law, that we might receive adoption to sonship. Because you are his sons, God sent the Spirit of his Son into our hearts, the Spirit who calls out, "Abba, Father." So you are no longer a slave, but God's child; and since you are his child, God has made you also an heir.

GALATIANS 4:4–7 NIV

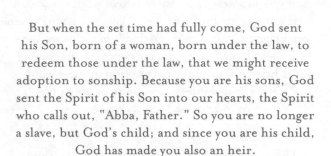

Everything belongs to God, and all things were created by his power. So God did the right thing when he made Jesus perfect by suffering, as Jesus led many of God's children to be saved and to share in his glory. Jesus and the people he makes holy all belong to the same family. That is why he isn't ashamed to call them his brothers and sisters.

HEBREWS 2:10–11 CEV

Now you are the body of Christ,
and each one of you is a part of it.

1 CORINTHIANS 12:27 NIV

You were all baptized into Christ, and so you were
all clothed with Christ. This means that you are all
children of God through faith in Christ Jesus.
GALATIANS 3:26–27 NCV

"I will be a Father to you, and you will be my
sons and daughters, says the Lord Almighty."
2 CORINTHIANS 6:18 NIV

The Father has loved us so much that we are called
children of God. And we really are his children.
The reason the people in the world do not know
us is that they have not known him.
1 JOHN 3:1 NCV

There is neither Jew nor Greek, there is neither
slave nor free, there is no male and female,
for you are all one in Christ Jesus.
GALATIANS 3:28 ESV

All beings in heaven and on earth
receive their life from him.

<small>EPHESIANS 3:15 CEV</small>

"If you, then, though you are evil, know how
to give good gifts to your children, how much
more will your Father in heaven give good
gifts to those who ask him!"

<small>MATTHEW 7:11 NIV</small>

But his father said to the servants, "Hurry and
bring the best clothes and put them on him.
Give him a ring for his finger and sandals for his feet.
Get the best calf and prepare it, so we can eat and
celebrate. This son of mine was dead, but has now
come back to life. He was lost and has now
been found." And they began to celebrate.

<small>LUKE 15:22–24 CEV</small>

"I am the way, the truth, and the life!" Jesus answered.
"Without me, no one can go to the Father."

<small>JOHN 14:6 CEV</small>

I praise you because I am fearfully and wonderfully
made; your works are wonderful, I know that full well.
My frame was not hidden from you when I was made
in the secret place, when I was woven together in the
depths of the earth. Your eyes saw my unformed body;
all the days ordained for me were written in your
book before one of them came to be.

Yet to all who did receive him, to those who believed
in his name, he gave the right to become children of
God children born not of natural descent, nor of
human decision or a husband's will, but born of God.

JOHN 1:12–13 NIV

A father to the fatherless, a defender of widows,
is God in his holy dwelling. God sets the lonely in
families, he leads out the prisoners with singing;
but the rebellious live in a sun-scorched land.

PSALM 68:5–6 NIV

"Do not be afraid, little flock, for your Father
has chosen gladly to give you the kingdom."

LUKE 12:32 NASB

In a desert land he found him, in a barren and
howling waste. He shielded him and cared for him;
he guarded him as the apple of his eye.

DEUTERONOMY 32:10 NIV

For we are God's masterpiece. He has created
us anew in Christ Jesus, so we can do the
good things he planned for us long ago.
EPHESIANS 2:10 NLT

Don't you realize that all of you together are the
temple of God and that the Spirit of God lives in you?
God will destroy anyone who destroys this temple.
For God's temple is holy, and you are that temple.
1 CORINTHIANS 3:16–17 NLT

"What do you think? If any man has a hundred sheep,
and one of them has gone astray, does he not leave
the ninety-nine on the mountains and go and search
for the one that is straying? If it turns out that he
finds it, truly I say to you, he rejoices over it more
than over the ninety-nine which have not gone astray.
So it is not the will of your Father who is in heaven
that one of these little ones perish."
MATTHEW 18:12–14 NASB

The Spirit we received does not make us slaves
again to fear; it makes us children of God.
With that Spirit we cry out, "Father."
ROMANS 8:15 NCV

While evil people and impostors will go on from
bad to worse, deceiving and being deceived. But as
for you, continue in what you have learned and have
firmly believed, knowing from whom you learned it
and how from childhood you have been acquainted
with the sacred writings, which are able to make you
wise for salvation through faith in Christ Jesus. All
Scripture is breathed out by God and profitable
for teaching, for reproof, for correction, and for
training in righteousness, that the man of God may
be complete, equipped for every good work.
2 TIMOTHY 3:13–17 ESV

No one can come to me unless the Father who sent me
draws him. And I will raise him up on the last day.
JOHN 6:44 ESV